MW00880385

Mercy—God's Covenant Assistance

Mercy is covenant assistance, and its roots tell us a lot about the nature and character of our Heavenly Father, and His commitment to His covenants.

God is a God of Covenant, so this book illustrates and explains what a 'blood covenant' actually is and compares and contrasts the different covenants God has made, and why He makes them.

God has repeatedly bound Himself with covenants. Why? Because He wants to bless people outrageously. Would you like to be included?

Jesus cut a very binding 'blood covenant' with His Father, on our behalf, at the cross. This book spells out just what is included for you and I and how we are to draw on it.

**The Covenant, of which Yeshua
is the Guarantor,
is entirely better.**

Hebrews 7:22

Mercy—God's Covenant Assistance.
© 2016 James Edwards
Edwards Family Publishing

ISBN-13:   978-15323342068
ISBN-10:   1523342064

The extract from Dr. E.W. Kenyon's 'The Blood Covenant' is used by permission from Kenyon's Gospel Publishing Society. P.O.Box 973, Lynnwood, WA 98046-0973, USA.
ISBN-10: 1577700155
ISBN-13: 978-1577700159

Edited by Lisa Lickel.
Cover Photo by Ernst Meyer
Printed by CreateSpace, and Amazon.com Company.
Available from Amazon.com and other book stores.
Available on Kindle and other devices.

Published by Edwards Family Publishing:
www.facebook.com/Edwards-Family-Publishing-
610790572281939

Acknowledgements

Thank you, Heavenly Father, for choosing to cut covenant with man—for recognising our difficulty at taking you at your amazing word, and cutting a covenant with us that we may have this re-assurance.

Thank you, Jesus, for going through with it on our behalf and showing us your Father's heart.

Thank you, Holy Spirit, for revealing Father's heart to us.

Many wonderful men and women of God have contributed to this. While I choose to mention Dr E.W. Kenyon, Roger Price, and Bill Johnson there are many who have imparted wisdom and insight to me—for which I'm deeply grateful—thank you. Many are those who have listened to my stuttering explanations and encouraged me to pursue what the Lord has been showing to me—thank you all so much.

And I must also add Carole Brown, Joanne Marsh, Nicola Taylor, Randy Kirk, Heather Tremblay, and Lorilyn Roberts for Beta Reading the various drafts and highlighting areas for improvement. This is just so much better for your advice, support and especially your encouragement. And a very big thank you too for Lisa Lickel for your amazing suggestions, attention to detail and invaluable assistance in turning a manuscript into a book.

Hebrews 6:16-19

Men verily swear by the greater: and an oath for confirmation is to them an end of all strife.

Wherein God, willing more abundantly to show unto the heirs of promise the immutability of his counsel, confirmed it by an oath:

That by two immutable things, in which it was impossible for God to lie, we might have a strong consolation, who have fled for refuge to lay hold upon the hope set before us:

Which hope we have as an anchor of the soul, both sure and steadfast, and which entereth into that within the veil.

Table of Contents

Introduction

There is a very important side of our Heavenly Father that has been very largely lost through the centuries: the weight He places on Blood Covenant. Few have delved into understanding this facet of His character and dealings with mankind. The more I have studied and dug into this, the greater the weight I place in what I find. It is a mighty key that unlocks the promises, plans and purposes He has for each one of us. It reveals so much about His Father's heart and love for us, His children, and His eternal plans to redeem this world. Understanding Blood Covenant is hugely fundamental to understanding so much of His relationship and dealings with man, and how He longs to relate with you and me.

From computer games we have many pictures of keys; they are no longer those funny-shaped metal things we insert in a lock and twist. It may be some hard won secret knowledge that, applied in a particular way, unlocks the riches of that level of the game. It may be a particular way or sequence of doing things that unravels and hence, unlocks the prize. The key may be a number combination we punch in or twist the safe's locking dial to open. So whatever your picture of a key you are holding in your imagination, this one is spelled M-E-R-C-Y. But that doesn't tell you much about what it is that the key unlocks, remembering that you only lock up something of value.

While this book outlines the key, it also outlines something of what it unlocks. I can only hope to sketch out a framework as so many of the details are unique for each of us. What our loving Heavenly Father has hidden for you is different from what He has hidden for me. They are not hidden *from* us, but like Easter eggs for our children's Easter egg hunt, hidden *for* us. He has so lovingly hidden priceless treasures for us to find, priceless facets of His character for us to explore, unimaginable depths of love for us to fathom. Perhaps even more amazing is His trust in us to accomplish what He plans and purposes; His longing to empower us with His Spirit to reveal Himself to this world, for which He paid such a high price.

Now somehow He has to do this without destroying us in the process. In the midst of our chaos, our weakness, our selfishness, He has to so grow our maturity, our character and our love that our uniqueness can shine out with an ever-increasing weight of His Glory without us crumbling or going off track as a result.

It is my hope and prayer that this will get you started and equip you with the basis and framework of a viewpoint that you can stand on through the storms of life. To enrich and deepen your faith could be reason enough, but that is not my purpose. My purpose here is to empower you with a vision of Papa God's amazing love and provision for you. Such a vision will equip you with essential tools to tear down demonic strongholds with faith and power to usher in the Kingdom of Heaven in their place and the rule of our servant King, Jesus.

But there is even more than this. I want to look at Covenant, and those covenant promises through the perspective of honour to the one who paid such a high price to make them available to us. He left the royal palace and throne room of the universe and humbled Himself—even to the cross. Without His cutting Covenant with Father, on our behalf, none of these promises would be available. So if we are to honour that sacrifice, we cannot stand idly by wailing over our unworthiness, or sin, but rather we are called to stand as His covenant, Blood-bought partners, in the strength of His might, forgiven and clothed in His Righteousness and demonstrate His

2

Goodness. The weaker, the poorer we are, the greater the Glory that shines out. "For we have this treasure in earthen vessels, that the excellency may be of God."[1]

Mercy and covenant reveal so much about the heart of our Heavenly Father. His reason for cutting covenant and the depth and commitment He has to fulfilling His covenants reveal the value He places on us and the richness of life to which He has called us. Mercy tells us so much about what His Kingdom looks like and how it operates and functions—which has to be a reflection of the King Himself.

So may this open your eyes to the 'more' that the Lord longs for you to have and to walk in. The dreams and details will be unique to you, your personality and your situation, but His provision is boundless and free...

For me it began with my search for the true meaning behind the word 'Mercy'. The roots were not what I expected, but revealed something very different to our contemporary usage. It is so different I include a strange chapter about moving ancient landmarks—is it really permissible to change the meaning of such a landmark word? But my search revealed an amazing, consistent portrait of our Heavenly Father's nature, tied to very binding and costly Blood Covenants. This is Part 1.

So what is a 'covenant' and what does a 'blood covenant' look like? What does 'cutting covenant' mean in the 21st Century? How can God cut covenant with you and me, and why? These are the issues addressed in Part 2.

But, as Christians, we are partakers of the 'New Covenant'. So Part 3 looks at how our 'New Covenant' was inaugurated.

Follow me on the trail to see what was covered as this covenant was cut. In the light of this, our response is spelled out in Part 4, together with just how we invoke it. We have such a vital and important part to play in this New Covenant—to

---

[1] 2 Corinthians 4:7

3

invoke it and to rest our lives and hearts on it. But anything which carries 'responsibility' with it, then has some consequences where we fail to play our part, so yes, I've included some warnings to hopefully help you avoid the worst of the pitfalls. But what are its terms and conditions, what does it cover? What are the blessings of the New Covenant and where can you find a list of them? The answers to these questions make up Part 5.

Before we switch to Old Covenant covenants (promises), one role is pivotal throughout. One book of the Bible is dedicated to portraying the New in the terms of the Old. The letter to the Hebrews paints just such a picture with Jesus clearly portrayed as the fulfilment of Our High Priest for ever. Part 6 is dedicated to the letter to the Hebrews; this bridge between the Old and the New.

In my study of the covenants God has made with man, I was somewhat surprised to find that those He cut with the Patriarchs Abraham, Isaac, and Jacob, have rather more similarity with our New Covenant than with the Mosaic Old Covenant. So I have included these here, with the similarities spelled out. And while the blessings may look a long way off in your life, we can look at these patriarchs and see how God did indeed take impossible situations and fulfilled crazily unreal promises, to the letter. And last but by no means least, comes the Old Covenant. While this covenant has been done away (Hebrews 10:9), its inauguration is amazing, and its promises remain. It has much to teach us and much that we must learn to draw on. So these are spelled out in Part 7.

Now, if I hand you a key to a geodesic dome, you may well wonder where the entrance is. Is each face a door with its own keyhole? Does it matter where I choose to enter? In this instance it almost doesn't matter where you start. Every time I try and order the chapters, I find them re-arranged to something different, and in practice it scarcely matters where you start, but start you must. And each face relies on those around it to provide the structure.

But why would a God who cannot lie reinforce His promises with a blood covenant? Was His word not enough? Fortunately, *His* book gives us the answer to that one.

I like to sum up each chapter with a little thought-provoking conclusion, which I hope you will allow me to do even for the Introduction.

Conclusion

God is good ALL the time. "He is gooder than we think— so we need to change the way we think." –Paul Manwaring

I hope this book helps change the way you think, and especially the way you see and relate to your Heavenly Father.

Part 1: Mercy—the Key

Chapter 1
Covenant Assistance—Mercy

A covenant is a very binding, reciprocal agreement between two parties. So, there will be times when covenant assistance is necessary, and you need to call on your covenant partner for help. The Hebrew word for covenant assistance is *hesed*, which is what has been translated as Mercy. It is a word with curious and strange roots that illustrate powerfully and wonderfully the nature and heart of our Heavenly Father, our Covenant partner.

When I entered into a dynamic and personal relationship with the Lord, the whole idea of begging for mercy really didn't jive. As we have to do with these things, I left it on one side for many a long year. I have heard it said that Grace is being given what we don't deserve, and Mercy is not being given what we do deserve. It sounded OK the first time I heard it—sounds logical. But now I know better, and I'd want to shout out, "NO IT DOESN'T". Then I was reading that wonderful story of Jehoshaphat instructing the worshippers on what to sing in their worship as they lead out in front of the troops facing this vast army that had come out to attack them:

> 2 Chronicles 20:21 Jehoshaphat appointed singers unto the LORD, and that should praise the beauty of holiness, as they went out before the army, and to say, Praise the LORD; for his mercy endureth for ever.

Now for me that sounds a very strange battle cry "That they should praise the beauty of holiness" by singing "The Mercy of the Lord Endures for ever."

Try inserting our translation into this:

"That they should praise the beauty of holiness by singing "The not getting what we deserve of the Lord Endures for ever".

If you were faced by a rabble intent on killing you and overrunning your country, your home, your family, your children, would you really sing "The Mercy of the Lord endures for ever"? I don't think so! Not if this means "not getting what you deserve", then this certainly is no battle cry. It is laughable.

And so it was I began to realise that maybe in Hebrew this meant something quite different—and indeed it does.

The roots and origin of *hesed* go back to the word for the family's "household gods". These were the most precious items in your tent in the desert, and if the tent catches fire, the most important things you rush in retrieve are these household gods, just as, hopefully today, we would rush into our blazing house to rescue our children. Gradually the word's meaning migrated from the articles being rescued, to the act of rescue itself.

Just look for a moment at what is crystallised in this origin.

It is an act of rescuing something very precious—in fact, the most precious thing.[1]

But let us come back to the roots of this word *hesed*.

So firstly it is an Act. It is ACTION. This is not passive. First and foremost, this is *doing* something about a drastic and damaging situation.

It is towards something very special, precious and highly valued. But it is more than that—it is towards the very title to an

---

[1] I have since discovered that in this culture the owner of the household gods held the birthright. This is behind Rachel's taking Laban's household gods when Jacob finally decided to leave Laban, in Genesis 31. Fascinating detail, but not crucial here so I have placed it as an Appendix. See Appendix 1.

inheritance—something much more valuable than it appears.

It is an act with little thought for the consequences on the rescuer. They may well get seriously burned, maimed and disfigured, or even die in the process.

There is a sense of desperation, of "failure-is-not-an-option", about such an action.

Its roots are surrounded by billows of smoke and fire, burning the skin, searing the lungs.

This is Mercy!

This is covenant assistance. This was that loyalty one was obliged to give on behalf of a covenant partner. This too could be very costly.

When we study Blood Covenant in a later chapter, the key parameter that stands out is its binding nature. Many deadly curses are heaped upon anyone failing to uphold their side of a covenant, especially a blood covenant.

Is our El Shaddai, the God-of-more-than-enough, going to be able to be of any assistance?

> Ephesians 3:20 Now unto him that is able to do exceeding abundantly above all that we ask or think, according to the power that worketh in us.

We can scarcely glimpse at the closeness and intimacy of the relationship between each member of the Trinity that Our Heavenly Father put on the line out of His love for you and me. We assess the value of something, by the amount someone is prepared to pay for it. This is the measure of the value He places on you and me, the price paid for us was that He gave His Son.

Now, if you are in dire need of covenant assistance right this minute and can't wait to read the chapters in between because you are that hungry for your miracle, then you'd better jump straight to Part 4, 'Invoking the New Covenant'.

Conclusion

This is the fiery passionate heart of our Heavenly Daddy. Failure is not an option.

> Romans 8:32 He who spared not His own Son, but delivered him up for us all, how will He not with Him also freely give us all things?

He has outrageous plans to give you and me a future and a hope—a future and a hope brighter than our wildest dreams.

He so wants us to have this that He bound Himself with a blood covenant so there would be absolutely no doubting His intentions.

Chapter 2
Re-establishing the Landmark

A re-examination of such a basic word as "Mercy" may look like I am picking up and moving one of those ancient boundary stones put there for our clear guidance, particularly when I completely redefine its meaning. Am I really allowed to so completely redefine such a boundary stone?

> Deuteronomy 19:14 Thou shalt not remove thy neighbour's landmark, which they of old time have set in thine inheritance, which thou shalt inherit in the land that the LORD thy God giveth thee to possess it.

> Deuteronomy 27:17 Cursed be he that removeth his neighbour's landmark. And all the people shall say, Amen.

These verses recount dire cursing on anyone moving their neighbour's boundary stone.

> Proverbs 22:28 Remove not the ancient landmark, which thy fathers have set.

But rather—over time—some of the old boundary stones have been left to brambles and creepers so that their original designation has long since got lost. Time has allowed their original meaning and significance to become obscured, and finally in stagnation to become something completely opposite to their original intent.

It is time to clear the ground, dig out the plant growth,

clean down the stones and re-examine their ancient writing.

Let us restore the boundary markers and give them back their rightful prominence. Perhaps the sister to Mercy is 'Grace'; another clear boundary stone for our guidance. Joseph Prince, in *Destined to Reign*, has done a wonderful job clearing the debris and clutter and removing the verdigris in his clear exposition of the nature, the importance, the power and significance of "Grace". There is something about our human nature that has such difficulty in receiving something for free— we always feel we have to pay in some way or other. But Grace is, and always will be, God's amazing and wonderful riches given to us least deserving, absolutely freely. Indeed, we have no currency with any value with which to pay. On top of this, to be counted as righteous simply on the basis of our faith in Jesus and what He has won for us, is wonder indeed. Grace is a mighty and powerful cornerstone of our relationship with our Heavenly Father, as too is 'Mercy'.

May I do similar justice to "Mercy", and in particular, to that phrase "The Mercy of the Lord Endures forever." How often do Grace and Mercy go hand in hand such as in Psalm 23 that these two "shall follow thee all the days of thy life".

Both Grace and Mercy describe very precious aspects of our Heavenly Father's character and nature in His approach and love of humanity—each and every one of us. So this is indeed Holy Ground exploring His very character, His heart and His nature.

I feel this boundary stone has been hidden for far too long—

May the Grace of the Holy Spirit direct my writing, and direct your understanding to appreciate His nature and His love towards you, as exemplified by this mighty landmark:

"His Mercy Endures Forever", Psalm 136

I feel here rather like a gold miner who has been scratching away at a rough bit of rock, only to discover gold, and the more I dig the deeper and richer the seam appears…limitless.

I'm reminded of the guy who found the California Cavern in his hunt for gold. All he caught at first was a puff of breeze blowing a bush on a still day, and looking closer he realised he had found a deep cave system. On exploring it he found stalagmites and stalactites and other magnificent and wonderful crystals lining the walls. He registered his claim quickly, realising he had struck gold in a different guise, gold that would go on and on for a very long time; for just as long as visitors could be persuaded to come and see the cave system for themselves.

Or pulling from one of Jesus' examples—I feel like the person who bought a field because of the treasure in it, only to find it never grows anything properly, and then to one day discover the whole field has a huge beautiful Roman mosaic just below the plough depth, perfectly preserved.

Everywhere I explore, there seems to only be more to find. And while the picture appears completely new, everywhere else simply confirms its accuracy.

If I have bypassed nuggets that speak volumes to you, then do write and tell me. This impacts the way we see *everything*, I have only just begun the unearthing process and I think we need all the help we can get.

Conclusion

Deuteronomy 27:17 Cursed be he that removeth his neighbour's landmark.

Blessed be he who restores his neighbour's landmark. Out with those pruning hooks and the power washer.

Chapter 3
Our God of Mercy

But is His character really revealed in this description of the word "Mercy"?

Indeed it is. We can but glimpse at the relationship the Father had with the Son through the ages…. And His mission to planet earth—I think it is a perfect illustration of Mercy—a rescue mission, to deliver mankind from the kingdom of darkness. From before the foundation of the world, Father, Son and Holy Spirit had this planned. With a unity of spirit and purpose we can only guess at, their plans were made. The Fall in the Garden of Eden was no surprise that caught them out. But woven into our human frame was a likeness of Father Himself, with a strength and a will carefully framed.

Was it costly? Unimaginably so. The ultimate separation—with Jesus being made sin, and taken to the very depths of hell itself. There is indeed the smoke and fire of this rescue mission all over Him. If I dare think the unthinkable, it could all so easily have failed, if Jesus even once stepped over that oh-so-fine-line. Just how close was He to backing out in Gethsemane, we shall never know, but probably a deal closer than we realize. His risen body forever, Gloriously, bears the scars of His suffering—the cost of this rescue mission.

> John 20:19 Then the same day at evening, being the first day of the week, when the doors were shut where the disciples were assembled for fear of the Jews, came Jesus and stood in the midst, and saith unto them, Peace be unto you. And when he had so said, he shewed unto them his hands and his side.

Then were the disciples glad, when they saw the LORD.

But wind back a few chapters. Can you sense the "failure is not an option"? Jesus refuses to back down, but sets the whole of His will, and destiny, on seeing the rescue through to completion, knowing what it will cost Him.

> Luke 9:51 And it came to pass, when the time was come that he should be received up, he steadfastly set his face to go to Jerusalem.

Remember His anguished prayer in Gethsemane?

> Luke 22:42 Saying, "Father, if thou be willing, remove this cup from me: nevertheless not my will, but thine, be done." And there appeared an angel unto him from heaven, strengthening him.

Are we of any value?

> Ephesians 1:18 The eyes of your understanding being enlightened; that ye may know what is the hope of his calling, and what the riches of the glory of *his* inheritance in the saints, and what is the exceeding greatness of his power to us-ward who believe, according to the working of his mighty power, which he wrought in Christ, when he raised him from the dead, and set him at his own right hand in the heavenly places… (italics mine)

We are His inheritance. We are the exact parallel to those household gods—in that we have been rescued for a glorious future, seated with our big brother in heavenly places. We understand our inheritance in Him, but don't forget we are *His* inheritance.

How curious that so often the first occurrence of a phrase or word in the Bible sets the scene for it everywhere else. So where do we first find this link that our God is a God whose very nature is Mercy? It is in Genesis 24:27, where Abraham's servant has been sent to find a wife for Isaac—Oh, such a powerful parable of the reality of our God choosing a bride for His Son. And as old as the Old Covenant, this gives us this link between Mercy and marriage, so too we have a similar link in the New Covenant where Paul, in Ephesians 5, speaks of a man and wife being one flesh, but then says he is really speaking about Christ and the Church.

And the servant, awed at the immediacy of the Lord's answer of his prayer, with a willing and thoughtful girl—who was also "very fair to look upon" —bows in worship.

> Genesis 24:26 And the man bowed down his head, and worshipped the LORD. And he said, "Blessed be the LORD God of my master Abraham, who hath not left destitute my master of his mercy and his truth: I being in the way, the LORD led me to the house of my master's brethren."

Our God is a God of Mercy and Truth.

Conclusion

So are we the subject of a God who stands back from His warped and evil creation and "doesn't give us the judgement that we deserve"?

No, NO, NO—a thousand times NO!

Before the foundation of the world, He **set out to rescue us**, regardless of the cost to Himself. Regardless of the cost to His Son—He forever bears the scars; our names are engraved upon the palms of His hands.

He has not left us as orphans, for we are the very apple of His eye—we are to be the bride for His Precious and most Glorious Son, to whom has been given All Power and All Authority—in heaven and on earth.

Our Heavenly Father's heart is beating with a fierce love and passion in His love for you... *This* is Mercy.

Chapter 4
Mercy of the Lord Endures Forever

Let us look for a moment at the second half of this phrase—this rescue operation—"endures forever".

Is that like Yosemite's Half Dome, which has endured forever—well, half of it anyway?

It has stood there come what may, ice and snow, sun and rain and it's still standing—immoveable and resolute. Is this the picture of our God?? Sadly, for so many, this is exactly the picture they have of Him, and this phrase simply reinforces exactly that.

There's this demanding God who sees that we've failed and stands back from us—waiting

Oh, what an injustice to His Heart!

Mercy is an action—it is an ongoing rescue—and this action *continues relentlessly* throughout the ages, forever, regardless of the personal cost.

I'm reminded of Brian Johnson's song, "One Thing Remains." It sums this phrase up so well; how the Lord's love never fails, never gives up, but goes on and on. How His love is higher and stronger than anything we face; while remaining constant through trial and change. This is our Heavenly Father's nature. His love—His rescue—His redemption never fails, never gives up, and never runs out on me, but on and on, on and on it goes. Our debt is fully paid, and now nothing can ever separate us from His love.[1]

---

[1] Romans 8:39

Regardless of the personal cost, of the fire and the smoke, the wounds, the rejection and even hell itself, Father's nature is bent on extending Mercy, extending love and forgiveness and full redemption to you and to me.

> Psalm 103:8, 11, & 17 The LORD is merciful and gracious, slow to anger, and plenteous in mercy. For as the heaven is high above the earth, so great is his mercy toward them that fear him.
> But the mercy of the LORD is from everlasting to everlasting upon them that fear him, and his righteousness unto children's children.

Such is His commitment to your covenant rescue—He is plenteous in Mercy.

Psalm 136 is a whole Psalm exploring "His Mercy endures forever." I could easily include here the whole of it, which begins by confirming "the Lord's nature is good, for His Mercy endures forever." But it then goes on to include verses like verse 15:

> But overthrew Pharaoh and his host in the Red sea: for his mercy endureth for ever.

And verses 17 and 18:

> To him which smote great kings: for his mercy endureth for ever:

> And slew famous kings: for his mercy endureth for ever.

See the fierceness of His Mercy, His rescue, for His Chosen when they called upon Him? You really don't want to be on the other side and therefore opposed to His Mercy. Pharaoh and his host in verse 15, Sihon in verse 19, Og in verse 20, to name but a few.

Conclusion

On and On it goes... this love endures for ever...it burns for fellowship and relationship with us—forever.

His rescue, regardless of the cost to Himself, burns on and on, today and throughout temporal time, and forever through eternity—it *never* fails.

Chapter 5
The Lord's Battle Cry

So does this re-translation of this song that Jehoshaphat had the worshippers sing make any more sense? I think it does.

> 2 Chronicles 20:21 Jehoshaphat appointed singers unto the LORD, and that should praise the beauty of holiness, as they went out before the army, and to say, Praise the LORD; *for his mercy endureth for ever.* (italics mine)

Remember their position: "For we have no power to face this vast army that is attacking us. We do not know what to do, but our eyes are on you."

So their eyes are on their covenant God.

They are reminding Him of His covenant obligation, and are drawing upon His Mercy—His promised rescue.[1]

They are praising Him for His faithfulness to honour His covenant—when there is no visible sign of it at all—this is faith "calling those things that be not as though they are".[2]

They are reminding themselves of their covenant partner, and His nature and faithfulness to honour His Covenant.

They are reminding themselves that this covenant rescue obligation goes on and on; just as it was vital in times past in all of those stories in their history, it is equally true right in their now time, facing them at that moment, but is also equally true in the future whenever that rescue will be needed again.

---

[1] Deuteronomy 28:7
[2] Romans 4:17

At last we have a battle cry.

The Mercy of the Lord Endures Forever

> 2 Chronicles 20:22-25 And when they began to sing and to praise, the LORD set ambushments against the children of Ammon, Moab, and mount Seir, which were come against Judah; and they were smitten. For the children of Ammon and Moab stood up against the inhabitants of mount Seir, utterly to slay and destroy them: and when they had made an end of the inhabitants of Seir, every one helped to destroy another.

> And when Judah came toward the watch tower in the wilderness, they looked unto the multitude, and, behold, they were dead bodies fallen to the earth, and none escaped.

> And when Jehoshaphat and his people came to take away the spoil of them, they found among them in abundance both riches with the dead bodies, and precious jewels, which they stripped off for themselves, more than they could carry away: and they were three days in gathering of the spoil, it was so much.

The Lord is our God, and His ongoing, total and complete rescue never fails, and will never give up on me, or you. It is ongoing right now, in ten minutes time, an hour's time, a year's time—on and on, on and on it goes.

We need to get into a covenantal mindset. We have a covenant partner of unbelievable power to love, support, protect and cherish us and all that is precious and important to us. Old Covenant people recognized this, but our western culture has so lost this mindset it is frightening, and few more so than Christians.

Watch David's reaction on hearing Goliath's taunting:

> 1 Samuel 17:26 "For who is this uncircumcised Philistine, that he should defy the armies of the living God?"

Coming from a Covenantal perspective, Goliath was taunting not just the armies of Israel, but also their Covenant Partner. David was reminding people here (and himself), that Goliath had no covenant with God, as circumcision was the condition of the covenant. By contrast he was a man prepared to stand totally on the basis of his covenant, knowing God would come through because of His Covenant obligation.

Is there any part of your life taunting you, or in need of rescue? This is not a taunt against you alone but the one who stands behind that Covenant that you have with the All Mighty One Himself.

Is there any part of your body, your soul, your mind, or your sprit currently in need of rescue?

Is your job, your bank account, or your marriage in need of rescue?

Do you have any dreams in need of rescue?

"Ask and it shall be given to you," Matthew 7:7. Note that the tense of the verb here means this should really read "keep on asking, and it will keep on being given to you."

Take it to the cross and remind Him, of His covenant obligation, quoting chapter and verse of where it is promised:

His Mercy endures forever.

I personally would recommend that you then take communion over it—reminding Him of His covenant promise as Jesus asked us to, as outlined in Chapter 14.

But, what if He gives it to you in seed form or in some other not obvious way? A field of dead soldiers is pretty obvious, but if He gives you a seed, then this may not look at all like what you asked for. An acorn does not look at all like an oak tree, not even a small oak tree. Not least it will require you to recognise it. It will require you to plant it, and nurture it, and in time if you have valued and stewarded it well, it will become the answer. That responsibility is yours. You will value it all the more for having tended it so carefully.

If you are asking for a ministry of writing and He gives you the simplest germ of an idea for a book, guess who has to do his homework for this ministry to become a reality. Maybe you are asking for a gift of healing; well don't be surprised if you find yourself bumping into people in need of healing. And their situations may well not be convenient ones for you to minister into.

Conclusion

Press in to what He has promised—as this honours Him who paid the price for you to have it, **anything less dishonours Him.**

It is faith, not manipulating God, to press Him for what He has promised to freely give you, as "ALL the promises of God are Yes and Amen in Him."[3]

He cannot say "No!" to what He has promised; "He is faithful that promised." [4]

He who spared not His only Son[5] is your covenant partner.

---

[3] 2 Corinthians 1:20
[4] Hebrews 10:23
[5] Romans 8:32

Chapter 6
Goodness and Mercy shall Follow Me

"Goodness and Mercy shall follow me all the days of my life."

I love the 23rd Psalm; this is one of those, oh-so-familiar phrases.

I always used to think that these two wonderful angels would be following my every move, clothing me in the process with their anointing.

I now see this very differently.

What do you leave in your wake on the highway of life? This is my question.

Our driving, and driving style, is a wonderfully powerful illustration of what is actually going on inside us in our daily walk. If we dare to examine ourselves, this does show up and highlight issues in our hearts that are rising to the surface.

So what do you leave in the wake of your daily drive to work? Do you leave behind a trail of upset and frayed drivers you have cut up and pushed past? Or a trail of thankful-hearted people who you have invited to pull out in front of you, who may well have otherwise been stuck for many more minutes waiting for a space in the flow of traffic? I'm writing for my own benefit here as much as any other reader, as my wife will gladly testify.

What *follows* you is of your choosing. You set that up.

Forgiveness is well understood, that if we want to be forgiven, then we forfeit our right not to forgive others. Mercy is very similar: Matthew 5:7, "Blessed are the merciful: for they shall obtain mercy."

And in the cut and thrust of life, in all its busyness, it is often not an easy commodity to give away. Perhaps it is this that makes it such a powerful witness when we do. But if we recognise our need of it, then so too is our need to extend that to others. Freely we have received—freely give. So what exactly are we giving away? What exactly is this 'Mercy'? Here, it is something so very similar to 'Covenant Assistance', only it has an additional twist, in that this is assistance but without the covenant—just simply that they share our common humanity. Good manners and politeness can easily be mistaken for love, but Mercy is going another step—and usually what most would see as a step too far, and this is to someone undeserving. This is always by its very nature going to be costly.

Now James has a very direct way with words, and he spells it out this way:

> James 2:13 "because judgement without mercy will be shown to anyone who has not been merciful. Mercy triumphs over judgment." (NIV)

When we are aware of our huge need for forgiveness, we readily understand and appreciate the need to forgive others. We are well reminded of the exact same logic here, and just how much we are on the receiving end of God's Mercy.

Conclusion

Blessed are the merciful: for they shall obtain Mercy.

Chapter 7
Mercy in the New Covenant

Our relationship with Father God is now entirely on the basis of Jesus' cutting a New Covenant, precisely fulfilling the Old one and thereby rendering the Old obsolete. It has now been done away with.[1] So all of the New Covenant promises come to us through Mercy—this is covenant assistance after all. The New Testament is full of wonderful and amazing promises which all highlight and illustrate the Covenant Assistance we are mandated to draw on to bring Jesus' Kingdom rule to this earth. But first we need to be partakers and included in this New Covenant. When the Canaanite woman came to Jesus asking for Mercy in Matthew 15:22, no wonder He treated her so strangely as she had no part in the (Old) Covenant.

Mercy is a vital Kingdom attribute in the same way as Grace and Forgiveness. "Give and it shall be given unto you, pressed down shaken together and running over," does not just apply to money. This is Kingdom, and a vital Kingdom principle. Forgiveness, Grace and Mercy have been showered on us, so similarly we have no right to withhold them from others.

In the Sermon on the Mount, Jesus illustrates that Grace is hugely more demanding than the Law. Under Grace even to get angry with someone is as bad as killing them was under the law. So too is Jesus' call for us to show, and to demonstrate Mercy... As James highlighted, there is a strong inference here of judgement coming to us in return for our refusal to show mercy, in a very analogous way to Jesus' teaching on forgiveness. Jesus

---

[1] 2 Corinthians 3:11

gave Peter a whole parable in answer to his question as to how many times he needed to forgive someone; the conclusion of the story being: Matthew 18:34, 35,

> "And his lord was wroth, and delivered him to the tormentors, till he should pay all that was due unto him. So likewise shall my heavenly Father do also unto you, if ye from your hearts forgive not every one his brother their trespasses."

The attitude of showing mercy is so opposite to justice, but not one that I think about too often. But like forgiveness it returns freedom—freedom to the offender who can walk away and start over, or go back through the same cycle over again. And the more we realise our own receipt of mercy, and our own dire need of it, the more readily will we show this to others.

So many Kingdom principles are at odds with our natural human response for judgement and justice. In many ways this does not lessen as we draw closer to our God of Justice, and appreciate just how important justice and judgement are to Him. But our God of Justice is far from vengeful; He found a way where He would Himself bear the penalty, and make a way to freely extend Forgiveness, Grace and Mercy to all who would receive Him. But we are not God—though so often we act and think like we are—well I speak for myself here. Oh how often do I need mercy and forgiveness, so who am I to withhold these from others, in the light of what has been extended to me?

> Jesus, in Matthew 9:13 and 12:7 "I desire mercy not sacrifice," quoting Hosea 6:6.

> Romans 12:8 If it is to encourage, then give encouragement; if it is giving, then give generously;

if it is to lead, do it diligently; if it is to show **mercy**, do it cheerfully. (NIV) (emphasis mine)

How easy to show mercy, but grudgingly, rather than cheerfully and willingly. Nicely put, Paul.

Rather like giving—and the Lord loving a hilarious giver (2 Corinthians 9:7)—I think there is the same connotation going on. This is a useful reminder of just how different Kingdom attitudes and mindset are from the world's.

> Ephesians 2:3-8 Like the rest, we were by nature deserving of wrath. But because of his great love for us, God, *who is rich in mercy*, made us alive with Christ even when we were dead in transgressions—it is by grace you have been saved. And God raised us up with Christ and seated us with him in the heavenly realms in Christ Jesus, in order that in the coming ages he might show the incomparable riches of his grace, expressed in his kindness to us in Christ Jesus. For it is by grace you have been saved, through faith—and this is not from yourselves, it is the gift of God. (NIV) (emphasis mine)

God is RICH in Mercy.

> Hebrews 4:16 Let us then approach God's throne of grace with confidence, so that we may receive mercy and find grace to help us in our time of need. (NIV)

> James 2:13 Judgment without mercy will be shown to anyone who has not been merciful. Mercy triumphs over judgment. (NIV)

A warning from the previous chapter.

> 1 Peter 1:3 Praise be to the God and Father of our Lord Jesus Christ. In his great *mercy* he has given us new birth into a living hope through the resurrection of Jesus Christ from the dead. (NIV) (emphasis mine)

Conclusion

Our God is Rich in Mercy.

Mercy triumphs over justice.

Oh how we need to remember that.

Part 2: Covenant

Chapter 8
Covenant

A covenant in its simplest form, is just an agreement between two parties. It is a legal agreement. You put a stamp on your letter as a sign of your part of the covenant with the post office, and their part is to deliver your letter to the address supplied. The dictionary definition is "a promise to engage in or to refrain from a specific form of action, such as a restriction on the use of a property." However, a covenant is more usually an agreement based out of relationship, such as a marriage, or a business partnership. So just how binding is your promise, and what would be the penalties? The extent, the conditions and penalties may vary, depending upon the nature and form of the covenant. However a *"blood* covenant" has a much wider remit and is binding on steroids—from generation to generation—there is no wiggle room, and no way out. It is legally binding and it works in both directions—either may call on the other for assistance and help, to the absolute limit of their ability. Oh that I could take another word without the connotations and misconceptions and religious baggage that accompanies this word, but what else is there? Will someone please give me an alternative? We have a serious problem in our western culture in our disrespect for our word and our agreements—divorce and failures on mortgages are two ready examples.

Now stop and think for a moment—just how committed are you to the one-on-one covenant you have freely chosen to enter? How committed are you to your marriage covenant? No matter what happens, are you totally committed to give it your 100 percent to see it succeed? And for nothing more than that you promised… Are you committed to give and give everything you have and are—regardless of how it is received? This is covenant.

But an agreement is only going to be as valuable as what it covers and the ability, commitment, or power of the other to honour it.

A blood covenant with someone whose name and nature is "El Shaddai"—roughly translated as "The God of more-than-enough"—rather suggests that this is valuable. It covers "more-than-enough", and both His ability and power to honour His Covenant is "more-than-enough". But "more-than-enough" in what area, you may ask? In *Every* area of life from your finances to your love life, to your career and to your children. Oh yes—and to their children too. He is God—after all.

That leaves two other pieces to put in place for this jigsaw—what do we have to do to invoke it, with its corollary of how well can we trust His performing His covenant obligations? Just how committed is this El Shaddai to His side of this agreement?

His commitment to His covenant is quite unbelievable. This tells us a lot about His nature and also about His love and care for us. Never forget that He initiated it.

So as I explore the meaning and nature of covenant, I unfold the nature of that assistance that is so deeply embedded in the heart and nature of covenant. This covenanted assistance is 'Mercy'. It reveals so much of the heart of our God who chooses to cut covenant with man. Grace has its exponents, but Mercy, so very few.

Curiously, our God is a God of covenant. He has regularly made them. First with the Patriarchs, Noah, Abraham, Isaac and Jacob, then the classic Old Covenant with Moses and the people of Israel at Mount Sinai, and lastly at the Last Supper with His disciples, Jesus inaugurated a New Covenant with Father God on our behalf. How much you and I need it. This is not some nice addendum to our Christianity; this is central.

So, as an illustration of where we are headed, we have to ask the question, why on earth would God choose to make a covenant with man? Fortunately, the writer to the Hebrews has answered this for me, as I wouldn't have dared answer that one.

> As the Common English translation puts Hebrews 6:16-19, People pledge by something greater than themselves. A solemn pledge guarantees what they say and shuts down any argument. When God wanted to further demonstrate to the heirs of the promise that His purpose doesn't change, He guaranteed it with a solemn pledge. So these are two things that don't change, because it's impossible for God to lie. He did this so that we, who have taken refuge in him, can be encouraged to grasp the hope that is lying in front of us. This hope, is a safe and secure anchor for our whole being...

Or for those so familiar with the King James version:

> Hebrews 6:16-19, Men verily swear by the greater: and an oath for confirmation is to them an end of all strife. Wherein God, willing more abundantly to show unto the heirs of promise the immutability of his counsel, confirmed it by an oath: That by two immutable things, in which it was impossible for God to lie, we might have a strong consolation, who have fled for refuge to lay hold upon the hope set before us: Which hope we have as an anchor of

the soul, both sure and steadfast, and which entereth into that within the veil.

There are times in life when the Lord's Presence is tangibly real, and receiving amazing miracles, whether of healing, provision, revelation or simply His Love, is just so easy. For most of us, most of the time, this is not our experience. For nearly all of us there are times, sometimes short, sometimes long, when the opposite seems to be more the norm, that the Lord seems far away, and all hope has almost been completely snuffed out. Covenant is for these moments especially…

But the Lord never intends us to stay in that place, but to live each and every moment cognisant of His presence not just with us, but deep inside us. Many of the saints all down the ages will bear strong testimony that celebrating their New Covenant, as Jesus commands us all to do, played a vital part in maintaining that close fellowship and relationship. That British 'apostle of faith' Smith Wigglesworth and many others would do this daily, as I largely do also.

I realize my words conjure up a wide variety of pictures, and they are all valid. But for myself, I like to keep things simple, especially in my own home, so I take an all too brief moment to go through those fateful words of Jesus, and break some bread, and drink a sip of wine or something that will represent. In this way I remind myself and the Lord of His Covenant with me and me with Him, thanks to Jesus cutting it on my behalf. I really don't like shopping list prayer—but in most relationships there are times when lists have to be gone through—checks as to what still needs doing and that things have indeed been done. The problem really comes when this is the only aspect to the relationship—my wife and I would be sorely upset if our relationship deteriorated into just checking our lists. And so it is with our relationship with our Heavenly Father. But this time is also a precious time to remember those we love and those on our hearts, lifting them in thankfulness into His loving care, and calling on His Covenant assistance for them too.

So take refuge in Him.

And be "much encouraged" to grasp the hope that is lying in front of you. Hope feels, faith sees, and His Mercy, His covenanted assistance, endures forever. The assistance you need is on its way.

He is faithful that promised.[1]

His heart is for you, not against you. His heart is to pour out the riches He won, onto each and every one of us, in FULL measure, "pressed down, shaken together and running over."[2]

---

[1] Hebrews 10:23
[2] Luke 6:38

Conclusion

So why did God choose to cut covenant with man? Let us never forget we have some very special place in His heart. This for Him is a David and Jonathan love relationship. He understands our weakness, and loves and expresses His love for us in this amazing and wonderful way.

He wants us to be absolutely certain of His love, care, and commitment and the validity of His promises to us.

Chapter 9
Blood Covenant

The Bible Old Covenant, and New Covenant are both "Blood" Covenants.

A "Blood" Covenant is an extremely binding agreement between two parties. Most things we can exaggerate, but no one can exaggerate God's goodness, and secondly we cannot exaggerate the binding nature of a Blood Covenant. Blood Covenants appear to have existed in all cultures; between people, between tribes and people groups. Livingstone, in his tours of Africa, regularly "cut covenant" with local chiefs, and never ever observed these covenants being broken—they were always regarded with the utmost reverence and honour by all involved—regardless of the cost.

One of the greatest failures of our 'modern' society is the failure of individuals, people-groups, and nations, to honour their word. Divorce is so prevalent that marriage vows have little meaning in society at large. One of our most binding legal agreements is a house mortgage, but even this is being hedged around with steps to help people work their way around and out of the naked responsibility they freely entered. So we have seriously lost a real understanding of commitment to any legal agreement—and essentially lost a comprehension of the power behind this *most binding of all agreements*, the Blood Covenant.

In primitive societies the Blood Covenant is reverenced, never broken, and goes on through many generations. The blessings and the cursing are taken extremely seriously.

To quote Dr E.W. Kenyon's wonderful book, *The Blood Covenant,[1] Reasons for Cutting the Covenant*: "There are three reasons for men cutting the covenant with each other.

41

"If a strong tribe lives side by side of a weaker tribe, and there is danger of the weaker tribe being destroyed, the weaker tribe will seek to "cut the Covenant" with the stronger tribe that they may be preserved.

"Second, two business men entering into a partnership might cut the Covenant to insure that neither would take advantage of the other.

"Third, if two men loved each other as devotedly as David and Jonathan, such as Damon and Pythias, they would cut the Covenant for the love's sake."

The Method of Cutting the Covenant

The method of cutting the Covenant is practically the same the world over, although there are differences, of course. In some places it has degenerated into a very grotesque, almost horrible, rite, but nevertheless it is the same blood covenant. That which is practiced by the natives of Africa, by the Arabs, by the Syrians, and by the Balkans is this: Two men wish to cut the covenant; they come together with their friends and a priest.

First they exchange gifts. By this exchange of gifts they indicate all one has, the other owns if necessary.

After the exchange of gifts, they bring a cup of wine. The priest makes an incision in the arm of one man, and the blood drips into the wine. An incision is made in the other man's arm and his blood drips into the same cup. Then the wine is stirred and the bloods are mixed. Then the cup is handed to one man and he drinks part of it, then hands it to the other man and he drinks the rest of it.

When they have drunk it, oftentimes they will put their wrists together so that their bloods mingle, or they will touch

---

[1] The Blood Covenant – Kenyon's Gospel Publishing Society, PO Box 973, Lynnwood, WA 98046-0973 USA.

their tongues to each other's wounds. Now they have become blood brothers.

So what are the key elements that make up covenant, and more especially a "blood covenant"?

a. A definitive point of agreement (in this case a number of points)

b. Defined participants

c. Defined Blessings (and cursings in some places)

d. Conditions

e. A 'Cutting' ceremony, and mingling of the blood of the two participants

f. Setting up a memorial, such as the planting of trees

g. A celebratory meal

The result: A very binding legal agreement of great power.

Conclusion

A Blood Covenant is a reciprocal agreement between two parties to help and assist each other to the absolute limit of their capability.

I cannot over-emphasise here the binding nature of a covenant sealed in blood. Such are so many of God's promises to us.

Part 3 The New Covenant

Chapter 10
The Inauguration of the New Covenant

In the light of all that the previous chapters tell us about our Heavenly Father, and His love for covenant, we have to follow with an exploration of the covenants He has made. For Christians, I hope you will now want to dive straight in and see what this tells us about the covenant that we live under—our 'New Covenant'. We can then move on to exploring the Old Covenant and the Patriarchal covenants, comparing and contrasting them.

Before the Old Covenant is fulfilled and closes, a New Covenant is drawn up and established. For this we have to look at the Last Supper, where Jesus inaugurates the New Covenant memorial. For many of the details of the New Covenant, you must read on in the next few chapters, but for this chapter we concentrate simply on the inauguration.

Jesus sets the scene for the Last Supper by washing the disciples' feet. This simple act of humility sets not just the scene, but the spirit and tone of what is to follow.

> John 13:1 It was just before the Passover Feast. Jesus knew that the time had come for him to leave this world and go to the Father. Having loved his own who were in the world, he now showed them the full extent of his love. The evening meal was being served, and the devil had already prompted

45

Judas Iscariot, son of Simon, to betray Jesus. Jesus knew that the Father had put all things under his power, and that he had come from God and was returning to God; so he got up from the meal, took off his outer clothing, and wrapped a towel around his waist. After that, he poured water into a basin and began to wash his disciples' feet, drying them with the towel that was wrapped around him.

 He came to Simon Peter, who said to him, "Lord, are you going to wash my feet?"

Jesus replied, "You do not realize now what I am doing, but later you will understand."

"No," said Peter, "you shall never wash my feet."

Jesus answered, "Unless I wash you, you have no part with me."

"Then, Lord," Simon Peter replied, "not just my feet but my hands and my head as well."

Jesus answered, "A person who has had a bath needs only to wash his feet; his whole body is clean. And you are clean, though not every one of you." For he knew who was going to betray him, and that was why he said not every one was clean.

When he had finished washing their feet, he put on his clothes and returned to his place. "Do you understand what I have done for you?" he asked them. "You call me 'Teacher' and 'Lord,' and rightly so, for that is what I am. Now that I, your Lord and Teacher, have washed your feet, you also should wash one another's feet. I have set you an example that you should do as I have done for you. I tell you the truth, no servant is greater than his master, nor is a messenger greater than the one who sent him. Now that you know these things, you will be blessed if you do them. (NIV – on-line)

I'm sorry, but like Peter, I still don't understand. Not just my feet but my hands, my head, my heart, my mind and my memories and...

> Luke 22:14 When the hour came, Jesus and his apostles reclined at the table. And he said to them, "I have eagerly desired to eat this Passover with you before I suffer. For I tell you, I will not eat it again until it finds fulfilment in the kingdom of God."

Sense here Jesus' excitement at what He was about to enact with His disciples:

> Vs 17, After taking the cup, he gave thanks and said, "Take this and divide it among you. For I tell you I will not drink again of the fruit of the vine until the kingdom of God comes." And he took bread, gave thanks and broke it, and gave it to them, saying, "This is my body given for you; do this in remembrance of me. In the same way, after the supper he took the cup, saying, "This cup is the new covenant in my blood, which is poured out for you." (NIV)

For much of the detail of this chapter, I am deeply indebted to Matthew Byrne and his wonderfully sensitive word by word exposition of these critical chapters of Luke's Gospel in his book, *The Day He Died*.[1]

---

[1] The Day He Died – Columba Press ISBN 1-85607-430-7

This was a Passover meal, full of symbolism from beginning to end, carried forward from that first momentous Passover in Egypt, and added to over the generations. The meal itself parallels and illustrates so much of these fateful hours, but this I will put in the next chapter. For this chapter I simply wish to look at the places in the meal where Jesus takes the bread and breaks it, and then the cup.

Jesus takes these so familiar moments of the Passover meal and twists the familiar wording just ever so slightly. Unfortunately for the large majority of us, with no Jewish tradition, this is completely lost on us, as we don't know the Passover ritual or its symbolism.

First, He takes the bread. This would have been "when the apostles have drunk the Second Cup" in the ritual of the Passover celebration. They wait for the host now to offer the unleavened bread and bitter herbs, and the Passover Lamb, with the words, **"This is the body of the Passover."**

Jesus takes the bread, offers the thanksgiving, and gives it to them, but with just the slightest change in the words they anticipated. But the change is powerfully significant. "This is my body…" with all the nuances their minds shaped and conjured and associated with the sacrificial lamb. "This is my body…" a New Covenant, a new sacrifice to seal it, a new token and symbol to represent that sacrifice. This is now a new rite that will shape their recollection in the future. "This is my body, given for you. When you do this, remember me."

The supper is ended. Jesus and his apostles will mark the end by drinking the Third Cup—*Cos ha-berachah,* the Cup of Blessing, as it was called. Offering the Cup for them to drink from it, Jesus gives it a new significance. "This Cup," He tells them, "this Cup is the New Covenant made by my blood which is poured out for you." They have told the story of the Exodus. They have eaten the symbolic foods and the festive meal. Now they celebrate their redemption, with praise for God the

Redeemer and prayers for our ultimate redemption in Messianic times.

But there are clues here that people seem to have missed over the generations, and even Matthew Byrne is far too tactful to explicitly express. For the bread, Jesus says, "This is my body, given for you." Does this really mean the humble bread actually miraculously becomes flesh? Words can say such crazy things that we never meant. Can it also mean "this bread—the Body of the Passover, is a symbol of My body, I Myself am the Passover Lamb—all of this points to Myself, which is about to be given for you"? Or to put it yet another way, "This"—the subject of Jesus' sentence—is it the bread, or the symbol which it represented, within the Passover celebration?

And equally with the cup, can those words not equally mean, "This cup—for centuries a symbol in this Passover meal, was always a symbol of My Blood, which is now about to be poured out for you."

But what a difference these statements mean, to the "classical" interpretations that men have fought over for years.

But another facet of this is hidden there in those so often repeated words of Jesus: *Do this in remembrance of me.*

On the 11th hour of the 11th day in the 11th month we have our remembrance day, when we remember those that died in the various world wars. We choose to remember them, in our way, on this particular day. Maybe you would like to be remembered in a particular way—and wish to pass that on to your later generations....

Doesn't a dying man's last wish deserve extra attention and respect?? And here do we not have Jesus' last request of His disciples? "Knowing that the time had come for him to leave this world and go to the Father".

This is how Jesus requests that we remember Him. How often do we choose to remember Him in the way He requested of us?

By this act of remembrance we are reminding ourselves, and our Heavenly Father, Holy Spirit, and Jesus Himself, of that New Covenant—bought at such a price, for us. Do you need to avail yourself of some aspect this New Covenant—does a day go by that we do not? How much more there is—that has been bought for us—for us to enter into, freely, though the Blood.

Do this in remembrance of Him—His life—His blood poured out as the sacrificial seal on the New Covenant.

This is a Covenant Meal, and a Covenant Memorial. We do well to remember that the bread is His "Body broken for me"— to remember and to claim and stand upon those precious promises. Is this what Paul was alluding to in 1 Corinthians 11:27-30?

> Therefore whoever eats the bread or drinks the cup of the Lord in an unworthy manner, shall be guilty of the body and the blood of the Lord. But a man must examine himself, and in so doing he is to eat of the bread and drink of the cup. For he who eats and drinks, eats and drinks judgment to himself if he does not judge the body rightly. For this reason many among you are weak and sick, and a number sleep. (New American Standard)

If we neglect to remember this is a covenant *and draw on it*, then we are indeed failing to judge the body rightly—it is the body of the sacrificial lamb of a binding Blood Covenant.

Conclusion

Let us remember Jesus as He requested we do.

This New Covenant makes perfect those that draw near to worship[2].

So let us avail ourselves of what is so freely offered to us; let us honour Jesus and *Press in* to what He paid such a price for, on our behalf. We owe it to Him.

---

[2] Hebrews 10:1

Chapter 11
The Trail of the Blood

The rule of the Old Covenant sacrifice that we will cover in more detail later, was that everything was cleansed by the blood. So too we can follow all of the areas of life touched by the sacrificial blood of Jesus during those fateful few hours. Not everything was covered at Calvary. And before you cough and splutter too hard—remember Isaiah 53; "By His stripes, we were healed." Those stripes weren't laid on Him at Calvary, but earlier in the Pretorium….

> Luke 22:39-46 Jesus went out as usual to the Mount of Olives, and his disciples followed him. On reaching the place, he said to them, "Pray that you will not fall into temptation." He withdrew about a stone's throw beyond them, knelt down and prayed, "Father, if you are willing, take this cup from me; yet not my will, but yours be done." An angel from heaven appeared to him and strengthened him. And being in anguish, he prayed more earnestly, *and his sweat was like drops of blood falling to the ground.*
>
> When he rose from prayer and went back to the disciples, he found them asleep, exhausted from sorrow. "Why are you sleeping?" he asked them. "Get up and pray so that you will not fall into temptation." (NIV) (italics mine)

So here we have the first mention of the atoning blood—on the forehead of Jesus, because of the anguish He knew was ahead. The blood vessels just behind the forehead do a wonderful job of maintaining the correct temperature for our brain just behind, but as brain surgeons well know, the area right behind the forehead is that area that controls our emotions—no wonder this was blowing fuses. Apparently this wasn't a completely isolated example, as this is known to medical science as Hematohidrosis. Apparently Price Philip of Spain suffered this on realising the fate of his armada, and its failure to conquer England.

But for us—Oh what blessing!

He bore our anguish and heartache for us. All of our heartache is covered here by His Blood. No one can ever point the finger at our Jesus and say, "But you don't understand." Oh, but He does, and some... That is laid upon Him, precisely so that we don't have to—so that we can cast our burdens and our cares upon Him, for *He cares for us*.

But there is another curious parallel unfolding here. If we go back to Genesis 3:19: By the sweat of your brow you will eat your food until you return to the ground, since from it you were taken; for dust you are and to dust you will return. (NIV)

So the original curse from the garden is rolled back and covered by the blood, right at the start.

But there was more that we don't see during this time of anguish. Such was the turmoil that Jesus' heart ruptured. Again, this is a medically recorded condition, known to medical science, as a possible result of huge emotional pressure. With a ruptured heart, both blood and water flow from the pericardium (the sack that surrounds the heart) when this is pierced. Remember, after His death, when they pierced His side this was deliberately up through the pericardium, and both blood and water trickled down. If He was still alive and the heart still beating, then blood would gush out with every heartbeat. But with the heart stopped, normally just a trickle of blood would run down the spear. But this is not what the bystanders reported—both blood *and water* trickled down because His heart was ruptured. Indeed—our Jesus was broken-hearted— such was the weight of our sin—such was the hurt and pain of separation from the Father—such precious intimacy through all the millennia, broken at a stroke, as He was made sin for us.

No wonder then that He was unable to carry His cross to Calvary. The soldiers were well used to abusing their victims for crucifixion, and woe betides them if they overdid it and the person died before they got to the cross. Oh, how nearly they did just that with Jesus, but then they weren't to know His heart's condition.

Not only did Jesus know in the garden, what He was about to suffer physically—and the eyewitnesses descriptions in the Gospels are gruesome enough—but we can scarcely imagine the horrors of "being made sin for us" must have meant with all of its separation from the Father and later descent into hell. The weight, pain and cost of what we cannot see truly beggars belief. Is it any wonder His physical body could scarcely take the strain?

> John 18:2-6 Now Judas, who betrayed him, knew the place, because Jesus had often met there with his disciples. So Judas came to the grove, guiding a detachment of soldiers and some officials from the chief priests and Pharisees. They were carrying torches, lanterns and weapons. Jesus, knowing all that was going to happen to him, went out and asked them, "Who is it you want?"
>
> "Jesus of Nazareth," they replied.

"I am he," Jesus said. (And Judas the traitor was standing there with them.) When Jesus said, "I am [he]," *they drew back and fell to the ground.* (NIV) (emphasis mine)

Let us never forget that Jesus *allowed* Himself to be taken. The moment He said who He was (The Great 'I AM.'), *they fell back to the ground.* At any time through the whole proceedings He could have exercised His Sonship, but He *chose* to 'lay down His life as a ransom for many'. From here onwards we see Jesus choosing to lay His life down for you and me. At every stage, He never for a moment slipped into fear or into being intimidated, but strangely He rules each and every situation. This must have really wound the Roman soldiers up and added to their brutality.

But back to the trail...'

Matthew 26:56 Then all the disciples forsook him, and fled.

Only hours after their covenant celebration, and Peter's vehement declaration that he would die for his Saviour, they all deserted Him. So here the loneliness of desertion is covered by the blood. He knows—He's been there. Asleep when He wanted their prayerful support, and left alone right when He needed them. But there was another loneliness here as He "was made sin for us." I personally don't believe that the Father or Holy Spirit deserted Him for a moment, but this was something that Jesus had do as a man. Only a man could offer himself as the eternal, once and for all sacrifice on behalf of mankind. Sin above all separates us from our Heavenly Father, so here must have come a huge wave of rejection from that precious eternal relationship. Even after a lifetime of walking as His child we can only glimpse at what this rejection must have felt like, as we have only glimpsed at the intimacy they shared. And for us, in a measure we know separation and rejection, we are familiar with these things, but not so for Jesus. How much harder for Him to counter such a tsunami of something that was for Him completely unknown. Now, for us, they too are covered by the blood of our Redeemer.

The blood covered the march through the night to the house of Annas, and on to Caiaphas. All of the horrors, fears and terrors of the night are covered here by the blood on the forehead. They are not for you to bear, or to fear—here is where they are covered and paid for by the blood.

His command to us, over and over is "Do NOT fear."

From Annas He was marched to the House of Caiaphas where He was mocked, abused, and then "tried".

Here mockery and abuse is paid for.

The "trial" is worthy of more detail here, as Hebrew law spelled out very clearly many conditions for the trial of a capital offence. First, someone acting for the accused has to be appointed to put and plead their case. [I am not entirely sure that this was in place at the time of Jesus' trial. It certainly became a standard feature of Hebrew law.] Second, the witnesses have to be warned that they will be cross-examined and if found guilty of perjury become themselves guilty of a capital offence. Third, the case cannot be heard on the day before Sabbath. Roman law also adds that there has to be a full day between the verdict being given and the sentence being carried out. This is time for new evidence to come out, and to prevent hasty rough justice.

ALL of these conditions were swept aside in the Jewish elders' rush to see Jesus put to death; elders who should have been the very ones to see justice maintained, were so incensed. So injustice and failure of the judicial system is also covered by the blood.

But there is another twist to this—see the rush to have Jesus crucified…. Under Jewish law He would simply have been stoned, but no—the Jewish leaders wanted Him killed the Roman way, by crucifixion. They knew very well "he that is hanged is accursed of God" from Deuteronomy 21:23. This way He cannot be set up as a hero and a martyr to the cause by the mob, and is Himself seen as cut off from God. But the blood covers this too. If you have been placed under a curse, or put yourself under a curse such as by entering Freemasonry, then know this—Jesus has borne your curse—that which should be yours, He has borne it for you on Himself, on the tree. The full penalty of that curse has been laid upon Him in your place, the moment you acknowledge Jesus as your Saviour. You can walk free of that curse simply by acknowledging Jesus as your Redeemer—the one who personally bore your curse upon Himself. Such is the power of the Blood of Jesus.

Caiaphas couldn't find anything that would stick, and goaded Jesus to answer for Himself.

> Matthew 26:62, 63 Then the high priest stood up and said to Jesus, "Are you not going to answer? What is this testimony that these men are bringing against you?" But Jesus remained silent.

So, getting nowhere, Caiaphas finally charges Him under oath to declare whether or not He is the Messiah: The high priest said to him, "I charge you under oath by the living God: Tell us if you are the Messiah, the Son of God."

> Matthew 26:64-67 "You have said so," Jesus replied. "But I say to all of you: From now on you will see the Son of Man sitting at the right hand of the Mighty One and coming on the clouds of heaven."
>
> Then the high priest tore his clothes and said, "He has spoken blasphemy! Why do we need any more

witnesses? Look, now you have heard the blasphemy. What do you think?"

"He is worthy of death," they answered.

Then they spit in his face and struck him with their fists. Others slapped him and said, "Prophesy to us, Messiah. Who hit you?" (NIV)

So here mockery, too, is covered by the blood.

Look closely at the trials in front of Pilate, Herod, and then Pilate again and in each place Jesus was found guilty of nothing, but again and again He is denied justice, but maintains His confession before Pilate—as Paul records in 1 Timothy 6:13.

Let's look more closely at His confession to Pilate that's recorded in the different Gospel accounts. It builds a fascinating and consistent picture in Matthew 27, Mark 15, and Luke 23. They all comment that Jesus made no attempt to answer any of the accusations brought against Him, so much so that Pilate marvelled.

They all then record that Pilate asked Jesus,

"Are you the king of the Jews?"

"You have said so," Jesus replied. ("Yes" in today's English.)

Now Pilate's response is very clear from Luke's Gospel, "I find no fault in this man." And now he is trying to find any way out for himself, and grabs the opportunity to pass the buck to Herod in verse 7.

Matthew 27:24-26 goes on:

> When Pilate saw that he was getting nowhere, but that instead an uproar was starting, he took water and washed his hands in front of the crowd. "I am innocent of this man's blood," he said. "It is your responsibility."
>
> All the people answered, "His blood is on us and on our children."
>
> Then he released Barabbas to them. But he had Jesus flogged, and handed him over to be crucified. (NIV) (parentheses mine)

And of course in the Jewish uprising against Rome in AD 70—thousands were crucified—doubtless many of these, or their children—those who hadn't turned to Jesus. Those who did turn to Him remembered Jesus' words to flee Jerusalem at that time, so very few if any believers will have been caught and crucified during the uprising.

At His second trial before Pilate, John adds a further twist—

> John 19: 7 The Jewish leaders insisted, "We have a law, and according to that law he must die, *because he claimed to be the Son of God.*" (NIV) (italics mine.)

Pilate has seen and heard enough. He has been further warned by his wife....

> John 19:8-12 When Pilate heard this, he was even more afraid, and he went back inside the palace. "Where do you come from?" he asked Jesus, but Jesus gave him no answer. "Do you refuse to speak

to me?" Pilate said. "Don't you realize I have power either to free you or to crucify you?"

Jesus answered, "You would have no power over me if it were not given to you from above. Therefore the one who handed me over to you is guilty of a greater sin."

From then on, Pilate tried to set Jesus free, but the Jewish leaders kept shouting, "If you let this man go, you are no friend of Caesar. Anyone who claims to be a king opposes Caesar." (NIV) (italics mine.)

What an amazing confession. In the place set to humiliate Him, this preacher from the backward end of Pilate's domain has challenged his entire authority and worldview. So far from Jesus being humiliated, it is Pilate who is now the one on trial. Pilate is now desperate and desperately frightened—and Jesus has let him off the hook.

John 19:13-16 When Pilate heard this, he brought Jesus out and sat down on the judge's seat at a place known as the Stone Pavement (which in Aramaic is Gabbatha). It was the day of Preparation of the Passover; it was about noon.

"Here is your king," Pilate said to the Jews.

But they shouted, "Take him away! Take him away! Crucify him!"

"Shall I crucify your king?" Pilate asked.

"We have no king but Caesar," the chief priests answered.

> Finally Pilate handed him over to them to be crucified. (NIV)

But before He was crucified He was flogged and brutalized in a most horrible manner. "The Passion of the Christ" doesn't portray the half of it. Let's take Matthew's account.

> Matthew 27:27-31 Then the governor's soldiers took Jesus into the Praetorium and gathered the whole company of soldiers around him. They stripped him and put a scarlet robe on him, and then twisted together a crown of thorns and set it on his head. They put a staff in his right hand. Then they knelt in front of him and mocked him. "Hail, king of the Jews!" they said. They spit on him, and took the staff and struck him on the head again and again. After they had mocked him, they took off the robe and put his own clothes on him. Then they led him away to crucify him. (NIV)

My own personal belief is that every organ in His body was bruised here. There is no sickness or disease that was not covered by these 'stripes'. His refusal to be intimidated at any stage, must have surely wound these hardened soldiers up to merciless mockery and cruelty way beyond even their norm. The crown wasn't "placed" on His head, but rammed down with such force as to piece right through to the skull. "The whole company" wanted in on this one. And His blood covered them too. Metal or glass was woven into the ends of the whip that ripped out the flesh with every stroke—His body was a mass of bleeding flesh every which way.

> Isaiah put it this way: Isaiah 52:14 Just as there were many who were appalled at him—his appearance was so disfigured beyond that of any

human being and his form marred beyond human likeness— (NIV)

But in spelling it out for us in Chapter 53, He reminds us again, and again—it was for us:

> Isaiah 53:4 Surely he took up our pain and bore our suffering, yet we considered him punished by God, stricken by him, and afflicted. But he was pierced for our transgressions, he was crushed for our iniquities; the punishment that brought us peace was on him, and by his wounds we are healed. We all, like sheep, have gone astray, each of us has turned to our own way; and the LORD has laid on him the iniquity of us all. (NIV)

The price for our healing—of any and every organ—was paid for here. And as they led Him out to be crucified He nearly didn't make it.

> Matthew 27:32 again, As they were going out, they met a man from Cyrene, named Simon, and they forced him to carry the cross. (NIV)

So, on another Jew—a convenient foreigner—the blood came—and on the busy thoroughfare out of the city—all of the busyness of life, and of city life—the redeeming blood came and touched it.

> And as Luke tell us starting in chapter 23:32-34, Two other men, both criminals, were also led out with him to be executed. When they came to the place called the Skull, they crucified him there, along with the criminals—one on his right, the other on his left. Jesus said, "Father, forgive them,

for they do not know what they are doing." And
they divided up his clothes by casting lots. (NIV)

So right where they are actually crucifying Jesus and the
blood is spattering on the soldiers at their work, Jesus turns to
His Father and demands their forgiveness, and then goes on to
excuse them—amazing! I've noticed that it is so much easier to
forgive someone when you start making excuses for them.
When you start seeing the world from their perspective and
stand in their shoes—it is so much easier to forgive. Though not
stated, surely Jesus was praying exactly the same all through the
previous abuse.

But the law makes a big distinction between murder and
manslaughter—and He here is demanding that this is not treated
as murder, so in effect He is here setting Himself up as a city of
refuge1—for us ALL. "For they do not know what they are
doing."

And surely the soldiers at their work had no idea they were
crucifying the Son of God. So in that, Jesus was absolutely
right, they didn't have any idea what they were doing. They
were simply following orders.

We ARE Forgiven!

Let us examine crucifixion for a moment—it is hideously
designed to prolong the agony for as long a time as possible.
People could survive on a cross alive for many days. They
would cry out for their relatives to come and kill them, and put
them out of their misery—that was why the soldiers were there
standing guard. The agony was prolonged because the torture
was effected in such a way as to minimise their loss of blood

---

1 Numbers 35:11-13

through the whole process. Very little of Jesus' blood was spilled out at Calvary.

But there are strange things here that are recorded for us which I do not understand. As Jesus recites Psalm 22: "My God, My God, why have you forsaken Me?" how come the bystanders thought He was calling for Elijah? How come they knew enough Old Covenant to think of Elijah, without recognising the psalm? And if you stop and read through this crazy Psalm of David, when in his experience did he go through this? Surely this is as prophetic as Isaiah 53.

> Psalm 22:1-30 My God, my God, why have you forsaken me? Why are you so far from saving me, so far from my cries of anguish? My God, I cry out by day, but you do not answer, by night, but I find no rest, Yet you are enthroned as the Holy One; you are the one Israel praises. In you our ancestors put their trust; they trusted and you delivered them. To you they cried out and were saved; in you they trusted and were not put to shame. But I am a worm and not a man, scorned by everyone, despised by the people. All who see me mock me; they hurl insults, shaking their heads. "He trusts in the LORD," they say, "let the LORD rescue him. Let him deliver him, since he delights in him."

Isn't this exactly what the bystanders were mocking Him with?

> Vs 9, Yet you brought me out of the womb; you made me trust in you, even at my mother's breast. From birth I was cast on you; from my mother's womb you have been my God. Do not be far from me, for trouble is near and there is no one to help.

> Many bulls surround me; strong bulls of Bashan encircle me. Roaring lions that tear their prey open their mouths wide against me. I am poured out like water, and all my bones are out of joint. (NIV)

Someone who is crucified is hanging from the arms, so that his shoulders become dislocated, so this is a perfect description.

> Vs 14, My heart has turned to wax; it has melted within me.

I've mentioned earlier about His ruptured heart.

> Vs 15, My mouth is dried up like a potsherd, and my tongue sticks to the roof of my mouth; you lay me in the dust of death. Dogs surround me, a pack of villains encircles me; they pierce my hands and my feet. All my bones are on display; people stare and gloat over me. They divide my clothes among them and cast lots for my garment.

Even the Gospel writers noticed this last one.

> Vs 19, But you, LORD, do not be far from me. You are my strength; come quickly to help me. Deliver me from the sword, my precious life from the power of the dogs. Rescue me from the mouth of the lions; save me from the horns of the wild oxen. I will declare your name to my people; in the assembly I will praise you. You who fear the LORD, praise him! All you descendants of Jacob, honour him! Revere him, all you descendants of Israel! For he has not despised or scorned the suffering of the afflicted one; he has not hidden his face from him, but has listened to his cry for help.

From you comes the theme of my praise in the great assembly; before those who fear you I will fulfil my vows. The poor will eat and be satisfied; those who seek the LORD will praise him—may your hearts live forever!

All the ends of the earth will remember and turn to the LORD, and all the families of the nations will bow down before him, for dominion belongs to the LORD and he rules over the nations. All the rich of the earth will feast and worship; all who go down to the dust will kneel before him—those who cannot keep themselves alive. Posterity will serve him; future generations will be told about the Lord. They will proclaim his righteousness, declaring to a people yet unborn: He has done it! (NIV)

But look how it ends in triumphant assurance of faith— surely we see Jesus here holding His thoughts in check with faith, doing exactly what we need to do—to use the "word of God" aright[2]. Just as He did during the temptations in the wilderness, so too is He using the Old Covenant Word to keep His thoughts centred on His Father's faithfulness.

I hate the translation of that final cry "It is finished!" as surely this does not convey the meaning intended. For me this has to be much more accurately rendered "It is accomplished!" Yes, it has been finished, but oh so much more than that.

Fully Paid

And let no one conclude that Jesus died of crucifixion. Yes, He was crucified when He died, but that is not the same thing at all. A crucifixion victim cannot choose when to die—but our

---

[2] 2 Tim 2:15

Jesus did exactly that; He gave up His spirit. The price is fully paid—enough. He didn't need to hang there for days and days. Just as He had said,

> "No one takes it (my life) from me, but I lay it down of my own accord. I have authority to lay it down and authority to take it up again. This command I received from my Father" John 10:18. (NIV)

As Luke records for us, it was probably this above everything else, which marked out Jesus to the centurion in charge.

> Luke 23:47 The centurion, seeing what had happened, praised God and said, "Surely this was a righteous man." (NIV)

But what we don't see is the descent into hell, as Jesus paid the full horror and judgement—for us. We see a dead body hanging; a curse for us, but Jesus was made sin on our behalf and descended to the depths of hell. The devil thought that Jesus must have sinned somehow, for now he had full mastery and control of Jesus. The pain and the mockery that we turn away from in the Gospel accounts, is nothing by comparison to the descent into hell itself, separated from His Father, carrying the Full burden of our sin and shame, of our sickness, our disease, our...

But Jesus was not just carrying our sin and shame— "He became sin."

All that we should have deserved, He took on Himself, so that we may have life—eternal life.

John then picks up the story for us.

John 19:33-34 But when they came to Jesus and found that he was already dead, they did not break his legs. Instead, one of the soldiers pierced Jesus" side with a spear, bringing a sudden flow of blood and water. (NIV)

Had Jesus still been alive then blood would have squirted out with every heart beat, but as He was already dead, just a little blood and water flowed down the spear, just as John described. So this was the evidence the soldiers were looking for. But they got more than they expected—not blood only, but with the water from his broken heart.

And down to the letter, in perfect fulfilment of the Old Covenant, not a bone of His body was broken.

But we cannot leave the story there.

Let us move on to Easter Sunday. Oh, I do so love the words of that song "The Victor" by Jamie Owens-Collins. There's a wonderful live rendition of this by the late Keith Green on YouTube. This song so vividly expresses that Jesus completely fooled the demonic powers who would never have crucified Him if they had glimpsed at what would result, 1 Corinthians 2:8. Rather, they would have done anything to prevent it. It is now Jesus who holds the keys of death and Hades, having broken down the gates of hell, from the inside.

The Victor

Swallowed into earth's dark womb

Death has triumphed that's what they say

But try to hold Him in the tomb

The Son of life rose on the third day

Mercy—God's Mighty Covenanted Assistance For You

Look, the gates of hell they're falling
Crumbling from the inside out
He's bursting through the walls with laughter
Listen to the angels shout
Chorus

It is finished, He has done it
Life conquered death
Jesus Christ has won it

His plan of battle fooled them all
They led Him off to prison to die
But as he entered Hades Hall
He broke those hellish chains with a cry

Listen to the demons screaming
See him bruise the serpent's head
The prisoners of hell the Saviour's redeeming
All the power of death is dead
Chorus

Just look, the gates of hell they're falling
Crumbling from the inside out
He's bursting through the walls with laughter
Listen to the angels shout
Chorus

Words and music by Jamie Owens-Collins.

Just how do we *know* the penalty for sin was fully paid? That all *was* accomplished? Because He rose again.

But stop for a minute with me in the garden, and watch….

Jesus, fresh from the biggest jailbreak in history, sees Mary weeping because she can't find His body—she's distraught. And all of heaven is standing on tiptoe to catch a glimpse of their Mighty King of Kings coming to present Himself on behalf of humanity before the throne of Grace—ALL of heaven has to wait for Mary! The countless hosts of angels, archangels—indeed all the hosts of heaven, the Father Himself—all waiting for Jesus to comfort one young lady—and "He is the same yesterday today and forever." Just as He stopped for the woman with the issue of blood on the way to Jairus' house, one person crying out to Him in faith and love, stops Him in his tracks… and He is always this way.

> John 20:11-18 Now Mary stood outside the tomb crying. As she wept, she bent over to look into the tomb and saw two angels in white, seated where Jesus" body had been, one at the head and the other at the foot.
>
> They asked her, "Woman, why are you crying?"
>
> They have taken my Lord away," she said, "and I don't know where they have put him." At this, she turned around and saw Jesus standing there, but she did not realize that it was Jesus.
>
> He asked her, "Woman, why are you crying? Who is it you are looking for?"
>
> Thinking he was the gardener, she said, "Sir, if you have carried him away, tell me where you have put him, and I will get him."
>
> Jesus said to her, "Mary."

She turned toward him and cried out in Aramaic, "Rabboni!" (which means "Teacher").

Jesus said, "Do not hold on to me, for I have not yet ascended to the Father. Go instead to my brothers and tell them, "I am ascending to my Father and your Father, to my God and your God.""

Mary Magdalene went to the disciples with the news: "I have seen the Lord!" And she told them that he had said these things to her. (NIV)

Until He has presented His blood before the throne of Grace, the Old Covenant is still in force, so no wonder Jesus says to her, "don't touch me." The Old Covenant law was that anything unclean touching something Holy, made the Holy thing unclean. But under the New Covenant this is reversed, but not until this is brought into effect.

But later the same day, when He appears to them in the upper room, things are very different—

Luke 24 36 While they were still talking about this, Jesus himself stood among them and said to them, "Peace be with you."

They were startled and frightened, thinking they saw a ghost. He said to them, "Why are you troubled, and why do doubts rise in your minds? Look at my hands and my feet. It is I myself. Touch me and see; a ghost does not have flesh and bones, as you see I have."

When he had said this, he showed them his hands and feet. And while they still did not believe it because of joy and amazement, he asked them, "Do you have anything here to eat?" They gave him a piece of broiled fish, and he took it and ate it in their presence.

He said to them, "This is what I told you while I was still with you: Everything must be fulfilled that is written about me in the Law of Moses, the Prophets and the Psalms." (NIV)

But read carefully Jesus' words—"flesh and bone"—not flesh and blood—as His blood has been poured out at the Heavenly altar, and his veins are now filled with the Glory of God.

Conclusion

So whatever your state, whatever your need, whatever your position—it was covered by the blood. We are Redeemed—fully and completely—Redeemed!

But even that word scarcely conveys the enormity of what He accomplished for us. The full meaning of "Redeem" covers not simply the act of setting free, but the full provision and protection thereafter…

We are Redeemed!

YOU are Redeemed!

But if you finish this chapter simply "beating your breast"[3] like the onlookers, then you have completely missed the point of this book, and I have failed.

We are redeemed and adopted into His family to a relationship with God the Father Himself—all we have to do is to say "Yes" to His offer. All is by Grace, and for most people that is very hard to accept—oh how easily we slip into trying to work or earn something that is freely given.

---

[3] Luke 23:48

Part 4: Our Response to the New Covenant

Chapter 12
Man's Response

As I have mentioned, it is easy to read the accounts of the last few hours of Jesus' life and like the bystanders "beat our breasts" and return to life as usual.[1]

Maybe we go out and try harder to give ourselves to more love and good works.

But surely neither of these approaches are fitting.

We are not the Saviour. We cannot save ourselves. No amount of good works counts before "Him with whom we have to do"[2], but is simply filthy rags.

Some receive deliverance from their immediate need and walk away. Well—it was freely given, so ours to freely receive. It is not mandatory that we must then follow with slavish obedience. This is equally twisted thinking.

The simplest way is, as is so often the case, the one that so very few seem to see, and fewer still to walk. This is to recognise that we are forgiven, and press in to all that a relationship with the Lord is intended to be. This will be very different for each and every one of us—so much so that I scarce want to flesh out much more. But there are some key steps, and we can very easily miss them or trip up over them at any stage. Oh just how easily we are tripped up. (Well, I am, anyway.)

---

[1] Luke 23:48
[2] Hebrews 4:13

The offer of forgiveness is latent and there, as we look at the cross, we have to avail ourselves of that offer. We have to come and ask to be included—to be forgiven. Only *we* can do that for ourselves—you can't do this for anyone else, and no one can do it for you.

But we then have to receive that forgiveness. For some, that is particularly difficult. It is offered freely, and we have no currency with which to pay for it, so we have to simply receive. At this point, maybe you are wondering just how do I go about asking for, and receiving, God's forgiveness. As is so often the case, it is so simple that we miss it. I chose my words carefully when I wrote, 'you have to ask to be included.' Turn in your heart to Jesus, and speak to Him out loud—it really is that simple. "Jesus—I accept You as my Redeemer, please forgive me. I open my heart to You and receive Your forgiveness and love. On this basis, I forgive myself too." Our words are containers of spiritual power—very often it is vitally necessary to speak things like this out loud, and not just run them over in our minds.

But the offer is of so much more. Father loves us as much as He loves Jesus, and He wants to make each of us like Jesus—so that He is the firstborn of many brothers.[3] So He provides His Spirit to come and indwell to commence the process. Now some will wait until they are ready, or until they have cleaned themselves up somewhat. And instantly they have missed it. He is the very one to work that cleansing and changing process to achieve something that we ourselves are completely unable to do without His help. This is why all those self-help books always fail except perhaps for those very strong-willed individuals, but even here the stress induced is not godly. But the reaction to Love and Grace—is not pressure from the outside in, but a pulling from the inside out. And when we fail,

---

[3] Romans 8:29

76

we have an advocate with the Father who dusts us down, if we let Him, and urges us to try again with the same Daddy's heart for his toddler trying to take his first few steps. His longing is for us to invite Him to come in and take up residence within us—but He will only come as far as we invite Him, and only do in, and with us, what we allow Him to—we are the ones who set the boundaries, the limits, the restrictions.

Relationship. I have a problem with this. Like many men, we are busy doing things... Too busy doing things. Above all else our Papa wants a relationship with us, Holy Spirit wants a relationship with us, and so does Jesus. But how much time do we spend relating to Him? Most of us in the western culture are Marthas, not Marys, but it was Mary whom Jesus said had chosen the better role. Learning to relate to our Heavenly Papa is not an instant thing. Rather it is something to be developed and cultured—much like learning the ways of a person to relate to them. But our Papa delights in change, so just when we think we have learned what He wants, He moves the goalposts. When the Israelites in the desert were putting up their tents and to stay put, they never knew for how long. Just when they were nicely settled, the trumpets blew and the cloud was on the move again. Many times we will have to go back to where we lost Him, and start over....

And we too are surrounded by many voices, especially in our Western world bombarded by television and news. Somehow we have to learn to hear and recognise His voice through the babble. He is so ready to speak—if only we will make time to listen. But again, we have to learn to recognise His voice through so many—and the voice of encouragement sounds very different to the sound of a rebuke, which sounds very different to that of a suggestion, or that of a command. And sometimes maybe He would just like us to give Him time, not necessarily to talk about or through anything, but just to love Him, and have Him love us.

And may I add here—Papa doesn't *only* speak in the "still small voice." Oh yes He often does, but we are told that Wisdom (Holy Spirit) SHOUTS in the city streets.[4] Many times it is in the loud High Praise, giving Him Honour, Glory, and Thanskgiving, that I hear Him speak the most clearly.

Let us indeed "present ourselves as living sacrifices".[5, 6]

But even here we can miss it. He is not wanting us to simply lie on the altar to be walked over. It is a *living* sacrifice that He is looking for.[7]

And even in this walk there is one condition—that we forgive ourselves. We must forgive others, but we must also not forget to forgive ourselves too.[8]

Conclusion

Set yourself to relate to Father to give Him time to get to know Him, and open your heart up to Him so He can get to know you. He is so hungry to know you and for you to know Him. This is so important I have devoted a whole book to this— watch this space.

> 1 Corinthians 8:3 But whoever   loves God, is known by Him. (NIV)

---

[4] Proverbs 1:20
[5] Romans 12:1
[6] 1 Peter 2:5
[7] Romans 6:11
[8] Matt 18:21-35

Chapter 13
The Parable of the Supermarket Trolley

Imagine with me for a moment you are doing your Christmas shopping, pushing round a crowded store, until finally rather exhausted you at last make it to the checkout queue. And there in front of you is a single mum with three young children and two trolleys loaded with Christmas goodies that clearly she can only pay for by running her credit card even further into the red. So as they complete running the items through, you step forward and pay it for her. She has no idea that it was your Christmas bonus she was blowing—or just how tight your Christmas shopping is going to leave you—but in the midst of the surprise she appears grateful, and you get on with the job of loading your shopping.

Now imagine the thoughts that run through your mind when, as you complete your shopping, there, left in front of you, are those two trolleys. Some items that you remember would have been the children's favourites have gone from the top, but all the rest is there stacked up and left. Was she too embarrassed? Did she really not need all that stuff?—you certainly don't—you've got your two trolleys' worth coming through.

You can try and send your children out to try and find her, but that's unlikely as your shopping has taken a good while to come through and load up.

Frustration? Annoyance? Ingratitude? Bewilderment? Resentment?

Who knows?

As we have meditated on the Trail of the Blood, and seen that all aspects of life have been touched and redeemed for us—

let us never forget that this was for us—freely given. We can choose what we make and what we do, with what has been freely given on our behalf.

We may wonder at the cost…

We may wonder at the motive…

We may just wonder…

The Moravians put it like this, "to win for the Lamb that was slain, the reward for His suffering," and they believed the best way to reward Him was to bring souls to Him. So this became their Missions call. But He purchased much more than just souls. He purchased lives—He purchased LIFE in all its depth, variety, complexity, and abundance, and then gave it to us. He purchased *your* life, and He purchased mine.

We can pass by what He has purchased for us.

We can, through false humility, call poverty or ill health a sanctimonious "higher way".

We can see and say that these things are out of reach, as we are merely human.

We can take the one item—that is our most pressing need—when confronted by it, in our embarrassment.

Or we can press in and pursue Him and all that He purchased, recognising our need in every area of life.

Do we not owe it to Him in honour, to pursue ALL that He purchased for us, for our families, our communities, and our nations?

Press in to heavenly places, and bring Heaven to earth….

As He was being crucified He called out, "Father, forgive them, they know not what they do." As we identify with His crucifixion for the forgiveness of our sin, we must identify ourselves also as included in this forgiveness.

Surely—even as we are forgiven—do we not owe it to Him, to see ourselves as healed, whole, provided for FULLY in body, mind and spirit? And should we not therefore press in until this is ours? And should we not also press in to receive the mantle to pass this on to others?

> As the writer to the Hebrews so clearly put it: Hebrews 4:14-16, Therefore, since we have a great high priest who has ascended into heaven, Jesus the Son of God, let us hold firmly to the faith we profess. For we do not have a high priest who is unable to empathize with our weaknesses, but we have one who has been tempted in every way, just as we are—yet he did not sin. Let us then approach God's throne of grace with confidence, so that we may receive mercy and find grace to help us in our time of need. (NIV)

And if we are to obey His commission and heal the sick and raise the dead, bringing His Kingdom with us wherever we go, then grace and mercy direct from the throne of Grace is exactly what we and this crazy world needs.

> Hebrews 10:22-24 Let us draw near to God with a sincere heart and with the full assurance that faith brings, having our hearts sprinkled to cleanse us from a guilty conscience and having our bodies washed with pure water. Let us hold unswervingly to the hope we profess, for he who promised is faithful. And let us consider how we may spur one another on toward love and good deeds. (NIV)

There is a great exchange here: healing—by His stripes; deliverance—by Him being made a curse for us...the list goes on.

There is one I want to highlight, one we have scarcely touched upon—while the others may well defy the bounds of reason and common sense, this stands squarely across the path of the religious spirit. Fortunately this is not my idea, but straight out of Paul's second letter to the Corinthians.

> 2 Corinthians 5:21 For he hath made him to be sin
> for us, who knew no sin; that we might be made
> the righteousness of God in him.

Jesus—who had never known sin—was made to be sin for us. This is hard enough to comprehend. He did not just bear the penalty that should have been ours, He actually "was made sin". And for why?

"That we may be made the righteousness of God, in Him."

What on earth or in heaven does it mean to be "made the righteousness of God"?

Yes—Me—and You!

With all our addictions, sin, dysfunction, hatred, bitterness, or whatever: in Him, we are the Righteousness of God. This is an exchange indeed.

I would like to give some quick answers to this one. Oh that I could. So do you see yourself as a miserable sinner saved by grace, or the Righteousness of God in the anointing Jesus won for you?

Your Bible dictionary, or thesaurus, may well try and spell out the meaning of this word translated as "righteousness", but I can't help but feel there is a whole lot more behind this that we haven't dared to explore—it seems far too blasphemous, if we're honest.

But consider the exchange. Jesus became sin that we may have the righteousness that He gave up. Do we not owe it to Him to explore and possess our part of this exchange, which Jesus paid such a price to so freely give to us.

I think this will mean many different things to different people. Maybe in ten years' time I can write another book, exploring what I have learned.

In simple terms, "righteousness" would be "right standing before God, without guilt, or fear, or shame". And while this may steer us in the right direction of how we are to bring Glory and Honour to Jesus, it will lead us down many different pathways, as we explore the one "with whom we have to do."[1]

As always, we have the wonderful example of Jesus Himself, who modelled all aspects of what it is to live life for us, as a man. I rather think this is something we have to grow into, just like He did, in "growing in favour with man *and God.*"[2] (emphasis mine)

What would this look like for you?

Sure, it will look different from what it would look like for me.

The temptations in the wilderness give a wonderful illustration of just where this lead Jesus, in understanding just what it meant for Him to live out in ministry His being "the beloved Son of God, in whom God was well pleased."[3]

Each of these has at heart "*if* you are the Son of God…"

> Luke 4:3 And the devil said unto him, "*If thou be the Son of God*, command this stone that it be made bread. And the devil said unto him, All this power will I give thee, and the glory of them: for that is delivered unto me; and to whomsoever I will I give it. If thou therefore wilt worship me, all shall be thine."

(As the Son of God, it was His already.)

---

[1] Hebrews 4:13
[2] Luke 2:52
[3] Matt 3:17, Mark 1:11, Luke 3:22

> And he brought him to Jerusalem, and set him on a pinnacle of the temple, and said unto him, "If thou be the Son of God, cast thyself down from hence." (italics mine)

So you and I, the moment we accept Jesus' sacrifice as being for us, are counted exactly as He was before the Father. His righteousness is attributed to us; we are His child, in whom He is well pleased. We are orphans no longer, regardless of how much we may feel that way—we have been adopted into His family, with all of its rights and privileges, as well as its obligations.

Regardless of your outward circumstances—you are an orphan no longer, but adopted into the Father's family. Jesus is your Big Brother.

And yet we are higher still. We are called to share in and know what the Father has planned...

> John 15:14-17 Ye are my friends, if ye do whatsoever I command you. Henceforth I call you not servants; for the servant knoweth not what his lord doeth: but I have called you friends; for all things that I have heard of my Father I have made known unto you. Ye have not chosen me, but I have chosen you, and ordained you, that ye should go and bring forth fruit, and that your fruit should remain: that whatsoever ye shall ask of the Father in my name, he may give it you. These things I command you, that ye love one another.

So what does this look like for you? Will you live to grow in favour with God as His beloved son (or daughter) in whom He is well pleased? I wonder what particular things He has laid on your heart as your particular ways of pleasing Him—I wonder at your unique outward expression of that...

One aspect that has to be common to all of us, is a life of Faith—following Jesus our example who as always exemplified just what means— "For without faith it is impossible to please God."[4]

Conclusion

Pursue all that Jesus purchased for you. You owe Him that.

And in that pursuit, grow in favour with God and man, growing in friendship and relationship with God Himself.

---

[4] Hebrews 11:6

Chapter 14
Invoking the New Covenant

Are you in need of rescue?

I think you probably have a bigger problem if you *don't* think you are in need of rescue—in one area or another.

Jesus said that He had "come that we may have life and have it more abundantly."[1]

You are blessed indeed if you cannot think of at least one area of your life and heart that has no room for more abundance.

Oh, how much more there is! How much more of Him, His character, His Nature, His Kingdom, His favour and friendship there is to explore.

> Here is how the apostle Paul put it to the Corinthian church in 1 Corinthians 11:23, For I have received of the Lord that which also I delivered unto you, that the Lord Jesus the same night in which he was betrayed took bread: and when he had given thanks, he brake it, and said, "Take, eat: this is my body, which is broken for you: this do in remembrance of me." After the same manner also he took the cup, when he had supped, saying, "this cup is the new testament in my blood: this do ye, as oft as ye drink it, in remembrance of me." For as often as ye eat this bread, and drink this cup, ye do shew the Lord's death till he come.

Here is our Covenant Meal—our Memorial celebration of

---
[1] John 10:10

our Covenant with His Father, that He Himself had come to reveal to us.

Through the centuries "Communion", "Eucharist", "Mass", "The Lord's Table", has been celebrated and fossilised. Each denomination has given it a different form, and name, insisting that they are right, and fighting over the details. All the while missing completely is the recognition that this is a celebration of a binding covenant. Missing completely is the recognition of the supernatural Covenant assistance for *now*, of all that Jesus paid such a high price to give us.

For me, and I hope by now for you, too, the outward form is of little importance. Whether it is just you breaking bread before the Lord before your breakfast at home, or in a gathering of thousands in a much more formal setting, this is a covenant meal, covenant reminder, and Covenant Memorial —"do this in remembrance of Me".

And in this moment take your need of rescue to your Father reminding Him of His "Mercy"—His Covenant obligations to you, His child.

Don't you think this thrills His heart, to see in this precious moment you are looking in faith and trust to Him for your need—whether it is big or small—whether you even have the words for it, or scarcely know how to frame it in our sometimes such clumsy means of communication. Remind Him of His Covenant sealed by the Body and Blood of His Son—remind Jesus you are doing exactly what He requested you do.

So many of the things He asked us to do seem completely impossible—Go Heal the Sick, Cleanse the Lepers, Raise the Dead, and Love Your Enemies—being some of them. But this at least we *can* do—we can remember Him in this Covenant celebration.

And remind Holy Spirit of your love and trust in Him and His dwelling within you, to quicken the life, power and rescue of "He who Is More than Enough"—to invade your situation, your need, your world with His Kingdom realities.

> Lord, May YOUR Kingdom come!
> Your Kingdom Reign HERE!

In remembering the cost of our rescue, let us never forget to remember we celebrate an empty tomb. It was indeed fully accomplished, and paid in full—so that God raised our Blood Brother to the Highest place of Honour, and gave Him All authority and power in earth and Heaven, and gave Him the Name above every name. Indeed, we only know that all was fully accomplished because He rose again.

So while we remember His death, we also remember His Resurrection.

Conclusion

> "This is my Blood shed for you and for many."
> You are one of the many.
> "He *is* faithful who promised." (italics mine)
> He is the Resurrection and the LIFE.

Chapter 15
Warnings

An understanding and practise of celebrating our New Covenant meal with our Heavenly Father is a precious and wonderful privilege. But how easily does the form slip into pride of place over celebrating His Presence. It didn't take the 'Early Church' long to slip into that one, so why shouldn't we follow all too easily?

Jesus commanded us to remember Him in a particular way, which we do well to follow. But this is to take time out to remember Him—to remember what He gave up, that we may inherit—to remember and have fellowship with His Father.

Ultimately it was the restoration of that fellowship between us and His Father which is the heart of what His Life and Death were all about. The form may be helpful, or it may not. We may follow a set pattern; we may make it up as we go, day by day. Surely the important thing is to keep the main thing as the main thing. Keep the fellowship relationship and intimacy with our Heavenly Father central through the broken Body and Blood of His most precious Son, Jesus.

Beware what you dream for.

As Bill Johnson so beautifully puts it, we are responsible for what grows in the soil of our hearts and imaginations. What we think about, and dream about, will grow.

Who hasn't asked for a particular present for a Birthday or Christmas, but when it comes, find it doesn't bring half the joy that we expected?

Our Papa loves to fulfil our dreams. Big ones, little ones— dream carefully.

I hope I have emphasised that God wants us to be rich in

every way,[1] but do we pursue riches, or Him? Those riches are not to be spiritualised away, but equally, they are infinitely more than simply material riches.

Beware of lust in any guise. As you see the promises unfold—remember that while He longs to bless you to overflowing, beyond your wildest imagination, it is indeed so that your life may be fulfilling and fulfilled. But it can never stop there. It is also so that you can be a funnel from Heaven to earth to pass it on to bless others. It does seem to be the Kingdom way that we have to learn how to steward this properly for the flow to even begin.

I'm reminded of Mary pouring out her alabaster cruse over Jesus and the reaction and indignation not only of Judas but the other disciples too. In the midst of plenty, will the plenty destroy your hunger for more and for closer relationship and friendship with Him, or will it drive you to deeper intimacy in thankful-heartedness? Will the riches enlarge your vision of what you personally can change, of bigger things that you can influence with His direction and mandate to bring Heaven to this earth? It was in the light of her brother Lazarus being brought back from the dead that Mary poured out her heart in loving adoration.

But there is another very different aspect to Mercy that has dire consequences associated with it, and this is the need to show it to others. As Jesus put it in His Sermon On the Mount, "Blessed are the merciful for they shall be shown mercy."[2] The unfortunate corollary is that those who don't show mercy will find themselves facing judgement and a lack of mercy. Ouch!

[1] John 10:10
[2] Matthew 5:7

Conclusions

James 2:13 Judgment without mercy will be shown to anyone who has not been merciful. Mercy triumphs over judgment.

James 3:17 But the wisdom that comes from heaven is first of all pure; then peace-loving, considerate, submissive, full of mercy and good fruit, impartial and sincere.

Part 5: New Covenant Promises

Chapter 16
Our New Covenant Promises

So what are the promises and benefits of our New Covenant?

Firstly, there are many promises and benefits clearly spelled out for us in the New Testament—in the teachings and promises of Jesus, and further underlined by the writers of the different epistles. But what many miss is their inheritance by adoption.

There was a wonderful quirk of Roman law that prescribed that an adopted child cannot be disinherited. You could choose to disinherit your wayward son or daughter, but not your adopted one. Friends—we are adopted. We have a mighty, wonderful and wondrous inheritance. Any and all of the promises given to Abraham and his descendants are now ours, for this is the family into which we have been adopted. So ALL of the Old Covenant promises are now ours too—the terms and conditions fully met by Jesus on our behalf.

> Galatians 3:29 "And if ye be Christ's, then are ye Abraham's seed, and heirs according to the promise."

Now I can hardly here list all of the covenant promises of our New Covenant. But there are some I would like to touch on briefly, before we explore some of those precious promises we receive from our adoption. Now, if you have read this far, then I expect you to be very familiar with all of these Scriptures, but I am sure you will appreciate that they are all worthy of inclusion here for completeness.

> John 1:12 But as many as received him, to them gave He power to become the sons of God, even to them that believe on his name.

All that we need to do to get adopted into His family is receive Jesus. Simply receive Him as our Lord and Saviour. This has to be our starting point for everything else. And if you, the reader, have never turned and said to the Lord, "I receive you Jesus as my Lord, my Saviour," oh then don't wait another minute—no one can do this for you—only you can do it—it really is this simple. All I would ask is that you jump to the end of the book and message me on Facebook, and make my day.

> John 3:16 For God so loved the world, that He gave His only begotten Son, that whosoever believeth on Him should not perish, but have eternal life.

While we are instantly adopted into the family the promises are for here and now, and forever, too.

> John 4:14 But whosoever drinketh of the water that I shall give him shall never thirst; but the water that I shall give him shall become in him a well of water springing up unto eternal life.

Life—life and more life... Do you want *more*? I do!

> John 10:10 I am come that they might have life, and that they might have it more abundantly.

John 8:31 If ye abide in my word, then are ye truly my disciples; and ye shall know the truth, and the truth shall make you free.

It's very tempting to think that everyone else thinks like I do, but few are quite so close to being an addict as I feel. Am I glad of this one, that the truth of my world and reality is that He sets me free, free to choose? I still have to make those choices, but now I am free to do so.

John 8:36 If therefore the Son shall make you free, ye shall be free indeed.

Out of sequence but is such a counterpart to John 8:36.

Galatians 5:1 Stand fast therefore in the liberty wherewith Christ hath made us free, and be not entangled again with the yoke of bondage.

Acts 2:38-39 Peter said unto them, "Repent, and be baptized every one of you in the name of Jesus Christ for the remission of sins; and ye shall receive the gift of the Holy Spirit. For the promise is to you, and to your children, and to all that are afar off, even as many as the Lord our God shall call."

I think this really does have to include everyone who asks—no matter who you are or where you come from, you qualify for this; to receive the gift of the Holy Spirit. And what a gift He is!

Romans 6:23 For the wages of sin is death; but the free gift of God is eternal life in Christ Jesus our Lord. (ASV)

Yes it's free. It will cost you everything, but it is absolutely free.

> 1 Corinthians 2:9-12 Eye hath not seen, nor ear heard, neither have entered into the heart of man, the things which God hath prepared for them that love him. But God hath revealed them unto us by his Spirit: for the Spirit searcheth all things, yea, the deep things of God. For what man knoweth the things of a man, save the spirit of man which is in him? Even so the things of God knoweth no man, but the Spirit of God. Now we have received, not the spirit of the world, but the spirit which is of God; that we might know the things that are freely given to us of God.

I think this has to be one of my personal favourites. So what's your question? I just love this concept of the Holy Spirit searching our Father's heart and revealing His heart and those truths to us—oh what a privilege. Eat your heart out, Google. Holy Spirit is an infinitely more powerful search engine.

> 2 Corinthians 5: 21 For he hath made him to be sin for us, who knew no sin; that we might be made the righteousness of God in him.

The great exchange—Jesus was made sin so that we become the very righteousness of God in Him. Do you still see yourself as just a sinner saved by Grace? Or is this realisation sinking deeply into your consciousness—that you are indeed 'the Righteousness of God'.

> Philippians 1:6 Being confident of this very thing, that he which hath begun a good work in you will perform it until the day of Jesus Christ...

Now what has He started to do in you? He has promised He *will* complete that transformation.

> Philippians 4:6-7 In nothing be anxious; but in everything by prayer and supplication with thanksgiving let your requests be made known unto God. And the peace of God, which passeth all understanding, shall guard your hearts and your thoughts in Christ Jesus. (ASV)

Here's a garrison indeed. A garrison against worry, but we have our part to play. We are the ones who have to make our requests known to God with thanksgiving, which is our expression of our faith and trust that He will sort those things out.

> Philippians 4: 13 "I can do all things through Christ which strengtheneth me."

I can do ALL things? That's what is promised. Think very carefully what you would like to do. And then get to it.

> Ephesians 1: 3-8 Blessed be the God and Father of our Lord Jesus Christ, who hath blessed us with all spiritual blessings in heavenly places in Christ: according as he hath chosen us in him before the foundation of the world, that we should be holy and without blame before him in love: having predestinated us unto the adoption of children by Jesus Christ to himself, according to the good pleasure of his will, to the praise of the glory of his grace, wherein he hath made us accepted in the beloved. In whom we have redemption through his blood, the forgiveness of sins, according to the

riches of his grace; wherein he hath abounded toward us in all wisdom and prudence.

You are blessed with all the blessings Jesus won for you. How good are you at pulling those blessings from the Heavenly places into this world, your situation, and those around you?
Are you abounding in wisdom and prudence?

> Ephesians 2:4-6 God, who is rich in mercy, for his great love wherewith he loved us, even when we were dead in sins, hath quickened us together with Christ, (by grace ye are saved;) and hath raised us up together, and made us sit together in heavenly places in Christ Jesus:

He has 'quickened' you (Oh, I love that word.) and given you a special reserved seat alongside Jesus in the throne room— Wow!

> Vs 10, For we are his workmanship, created in Christ Jesus unto good works, which God hath before ordained that we should walk in them.

'Workmanship' is the Greek word for Poem. So you and I are His poems, created to demonstrate and show off His Glory and Lordship over this world, by signs and wonders.

> Vs 18-19, For through him we both have access by one Spirit unto the Father. Now therefore ye are no more strangers and foreigners, but fellow citizens with the saints, and of the household of God...

It doesn't matter what nationality it says in your passport— you are a citizen of Heaven. You have the equivalent of a heavenly passport, and no border officer can deny you entry.

Matthew 28:18-20 And Jesus came and spake unto them, saying, All power is given unto me in heaven and in earth, go ye therefore, and teach all nations, baptizing them in the name of the Father, and of the Son, and of the Holy Ghost: teaching them to observe all things whatsoever I have commanded you: and, lo, I am with you always, even unto the end of the world.

So if Jesus has been given All power, then His adversary clearly is left with none. And the corollary to this is a very specific directive to you and me. Directly tied to Jesus' Great Commission is this wonderful promise that He is with us even to the end of the world, and we aren't even close to that yet. And as if such a promise in such a key context was not enough, it is repeated for us by no less than that writer to the Hebrews.

Hebrews 13:5-6 For he hath said, "I will never leave thee, nor forsake thee. So that we may boldly say, The Lord is my helper, and I will not fear what man shall do unto me."

What a wonderful, wonderful, amazing promise.

Revelation 12:11 And they overcame him by the blood of the Lamb, and by the word of their testimony; and they loved not their lives unto the death.

Conclusions

You have been given abundant life. What are you doing with it?

You have been handed a search tool infinitely more powerful than Google, so what are you asking?

We are overcomers. Yes, YOU too!

Chapter 17
The Blessings and the Curses

So while you may have skipped over those familiar verses from the New Covenant, I hope you will stop and think what similar promises you also have at the forefront of your confession, from the Old Covenant. Remember, all of those promises made to Abraham and his descendants are yours by adoption once you're adopted into His family. For me, no chapter so sums up the blessings and the curses of the Old Covenant as precisely as Deuteronomy 28. But its opening blast is so brazen, we must examine it carefully.

> Deuteronomy 28:1 If you fully obey the LORD your God and carefully follow all his commands I give you today, the LORD your God will set you high above all the nations on earth. All these blessings will come upon you and accompany you if you obey the LORD your God. (NIV)

If you fully obey... Which of course none of us can—hence Paul's conclusion that "all have fallen and come short of the Glory of God".

But Remember Jesus spelled out so clearly for us that one key aspect of His life's work was to *fulfil* "the law and the prophets".

> Matthew 5:17 "Do not think that I have come to abolish the Law or the Prophets; I have not come to abolish them but to fulfil them." (NIV)

So He fulfilled ALL the LAW once and for all on our

behalf. So this means He fulfilled fully and completely the terms of this chapter, so that we enter into them through Grace—all paid for at His expense.

But like all of the promises available to us in the New Covenant, they don't simply fall out of the sky and we live with their wonderful fulfilment serenely every day. No, they come by faith—we have a part to play. He delights in us reminding Him of His promises—it is no "manipulation" to pull on His covenantal obligations.

So if your experience is not what is exemplified in these verses, please don't rail at me. I can look at one or two of these equally and wonder at my failure to pull His blessing into these areas of my life. Oftentimes His timing doesn't quite match ours. Whatever—the failure always has to be at our end.

So let us look at these blessings in today's western society—please enter into the spirit of my paraphrase and exposition here—but I really do think this is the intention behind each of these verses: Deuteronomy 28:2, "All these blessings will come upon you and accompany you if you obey the LORD your God."

I do so like the translation that says these blessings shall come upon you and *"overtake"* you. Now imagine you are on the freeway to work and your dream car is weaving its way through the traffic, catching you up in the rear view mirror, and finally gets behind you. In spite of your best efforts to block his every move he finally gets alongside you—he flags your attention—requesting you pull over. On doing so—he throws you the keys, saying—it's yours—all paid for, Shouting "ENJOY!" As he drives off in your old banger. In spite of your best efforts to stay ahead of these blessings, they still come upon you and *overtake* you.

Think carefully what you dream for.

Vs 3, You will be blessed in the city and blessed in the country. (NIV)

At home or at work—blessing everywhere. (And in between.)
Blessed at home, and blessed on holiday.

Vs 4, The fruit of your womb will be blessed, and the crops of your land and the young of your livestock—the calves of your herds and the lambs of your flocks. (NIV)

No barrenness anywhere—your marriage, your pets, your garden, your business, your ideas, your inventions, your plans, your dreams….

Vs 5, Your basket and your kneading trough will be blessed. (NIV)

Your fridge and your freezer—will be full—and they will last a looooong time.
In your bread-bin and store-cupboards there will always be more than enough.

Vs 6, You will be blessed when you come in and blessed when you go out. (NIV)

Now what do you go out and come in—in? Your car of course! (Are you driving your dream car?) And your doorway and drive will be blessed. You don't need to fear coming in to find the place ransacked.

Vs 7, The LORD will grant that the enemies who rise up against you will be defeated before you.

> They will come at you from one direction but flee from you in seven. (NIV)

I wonder what you fear most… no don't get to thinking, or like Job you will be inviting those very things to descend on you. The intent here is exactly the opposite. Whatever that may be—those enemies that come against you one way—**flee before you seven ways**—be it redundancy—divorce—bankruptcy—humiliation—loneliness…

> Oh, how much we need this one: Deuteronomy 28:8, The LORD will send a blessing on your barns and on everything you put your hand to. The LORD your God will bless you in the land he is giving you. (NIV)

Your bank balance and your credit rating—BLESSED!
But you do need to be putting your hand to something…and you will be blessed right where you are.

> Vs 9, The LORD will establish you as His holy people, as he promised you on oath, if you keep the commands of the LORD your God and walk in His ways. (NIV)

> Vs 10, Then all the peoples on earth will see that you are called by the name of the LORD, and they will fear you. (NIV)

And here is a taste of the reason—so that everyone around you sees that the Lord is the one who is blessing you and gets envious and drawn to Him—by looking at the blessings pouring into your lap.

Vs 11, The LORD will grant you abundant prosperity—in the fruit of your womb, the young of your livestock and the crops of your ground—in the land he swore to your forefathers to give you. (NIV)

Abundant Prosperity—what more can anyone ask for? And surely this encompasses far more than just direct material things, though clearly they are important. But this also has to do with dreams and longings, with favour and influence, with relationships and family, with the outcome of your efforts, especially in areas way outside of your control.

Vs 12, The LORD will open the heavens, the storehouse of his bounty, to send rain on your land in season and to bless all the work of your hands. You will lend to many nations but will borrow from none. (NIV)

The borrower is always subject to the lender. So if you are going to be free, then you have to be the lender; and this draws those to you to share and receive of the blessings He is pouring into your life and family. This has to be more than enough to liberally bless others—especially God's people—and His ministries.

Vs 13, The LORD will make you the head, not the tail. If you pay attention to the commands of the LORD your God that I give you this day and carefully follow them, you will always be at the top, never at the bottom. (NIV)

Now for most of us, we can look at those promises and laugh much like Sarah did in the back of the tent. But this is our God's love and intent for each and every one of us.

So while we skip over the curses which mirror those blessings but in reverse, there is one phrase we would do well not to forget too rapidly, down there in Deuteronomy 28, verse 47: (KJV)

> Vs 45-46, And all these curses shall come upon thee, and shall pursue thee, and overtake thee, till thou be destroyed; because thou hearkenedst not unto the voice of Jehovah thy God, to keep his commandments and his statutes which he commanded thee: and they shall be upon thee for a sign and for a wonder, and upon thy seed for ever.

> Vs 47, Because thou servedst not Jehovah thy God *with joyfulness, and with gladness of heart*, by reason of the abundance of all things. (italics mine)

Is your attitude and mine one of joyfulness and gratitude and gladness of heart to Him who has so liberally provided for us? Maybe most of these blessings have yet to materialise into your lap, then just remember He is expecting you to be demonstrating these attitudes *in advance*, as you walk out your faith, and trust in Him and His promises.

Remember the results of the grumbling of the people in the desert? They got what they asked for, but see how Psalm 106 records the result:

> Psalm 106:14-15 But lusted exceedingly in the wilderness, and tempted God in the desert. And he gave them their request, But sent leanness into their soul. (italics mine)

You really don't want to go there. Keep high on your priorities, a thankful heart and a thankful spirit—"We enter His gates with thanksgiving."[1]

Conclusion

Reference Deuteronomy 28:10, And here is a taste of the reason—so that everyone around you sees that the Lord is the one who is blessing you and gets envious and drawn to Him—by looking at the blessings pouring into your lap.

A second very keen point is that as these blessings abound through you, you are then able to bless those around you, especially the poor and needy, and you have MORE to give away—whether that's Joy and Laughter or $$, or...

In Old Testament times, if you ever wanted to start a quarrel, just talk about life after death. Paul used this to his advantage in Acts 23. Half of his audience did not believe in an after-life. So all of the Old Covenant promises are therefore very much for here and now. They are certainly not for some millennium in the future or even in heaven.

These promises are for you and for now.

---

[1] Psalm 100:4

Part 6: Jesus, Our Bridge Between the Old and the New

Chapter 18
Jesus, Our Priest Forever

If there is one book in the Bible that spells out Covenant and a Covenant mindset, it has to be the letter to the Hebrews. Here the writer was quite specifically and intentionally trying to illustrate that Jesus was indeed the promised Messiah, and all that resulted from His fulfilling of the Old Covenant on our behalf. Here is a letter addressed to a covenant-minded people of covenant realities—of New Covenant realities.

More than that, it is addressing the Old Covenant and illustrating how this is to be seen in the light of the New Covenant. This is addressed to people living very consciously in the light of the Old Covenant, and the writer is eloquently showing them how this is fulfilled by a New Covenant that renders the Old obsolete.

I'm so glad this letter was included in the canon of Scripture and handed down generation to generation. Some of its statements are absolutely outrageous. We so easily lose sight of their true meaning and value because of our familiarity with them in some old archaic language. Or we miss their power and impact through our failure to think through our relationship with Father in such a covenantal way. Here are statements to chew on until they reach foundation level in your heart and finally into your experience.

Largely because of our failure to think from a covenantal

mindset, the Epistle to the Hebrews does not make easy reading, especially for those not familiar with the Old Covenant and its rules, rituals and priesthood. Many of the traditional churches seem to have missed completely the message of this book in continuing a religious priesthood that carries on the Old Covenant model. Has no one told them this has been done away with, and *every* believer is now a priest unto God? For those unfamiliar with the New Covenant concept of 'priest' we do well to look carefully at the description of Jesus that the book of Hebrews give us as our role model. Remember this role is not done away with, or for you to leave to your pastor or village priest. If you are a believer, then this is your role too.

> 1 Peter 2:9 But ye are a chosen generation, a royal priesthood, an holy nation, a peculiar people; that ye should shew forth the praises of him who hath called you out of darkness into his marvellous light.

Yes—that includes even you and me—dog collar or no dog collar. While the traditional churches seem to operate with a priesthood fashioned along Old Covenant lines, the others appear to reject the term entirely, while their 'pastor' often fulfils much the same responsibilities. In both cases the New Covenant role of 'priest' is much misunderstood. As a royal priesthood we have much to learn, especially in the context of covenant and covenant memorial. Once again the book of Hebrews comes to our rescue with highlighting Jesus as a Priest forever; He makes a wonderful example for us to follow.

The Old Covenant for centuries had pointed out the harsh reality and penalty for sin. Once a year on the Day of Atonement the high priest offered the sacrifice to cover over the nation's sin for another year. As Paul puts it, this reminds us of our sin, and in so doing highlights sin's power over us.

What a difference under the New Covenant where sin is now blotted out[1], and "He chooses to remember it no more."[2] It is "removed from us as far as the East is from the West."[3] So do you see yourself as a miserable sinner? Straight out of the Anglican (Episcopalian) prayer book, and repeated weekly, is the confession of being a 'miserable sinner'. Under the Old Covenant that's about all you could hope for, but not under the New. You are called to have your sins forgiven. You are called to live in communion with Father, clothed in His Spirit of Righteousness, so that you are indeed the very Righteousness of God in Christ[4]. Now every believer is called to be a priest unto God. (Remember, this was God's original intention for the whole nation of Israel, Exodus 19:6.)

This illustrates just how so much changes as we step out from under the Old Covenant and into the New.

As we look at the New Covenant and compare with the Old Covenant, we have to ask, "What changed?"

So much Christianity is still fashioned out of Old Covenant principles and operation. As relationship with Jesus and the moving of the Holy Spirit fades into religious ritual, then unfortunately we move unerringly towards Old Covenant mindsets and practice.

So much changed at the cross, it is almost hard to find what remained unchanged. Animal sacrifice stopped but is transmuted to living sacrifices.

Now in saying that blood sacrifice stopped, everything associated with it stopped too. Jesus offered Himself as that once and for all sacrifice, and presented His own blood on that Heavenly altar. So too, the High Priest and Levitical priesthood

---

[1] Acts 3:9 and Colossians 2:14
[2] Hebrews 8:12 and Hebrews 10:17
[3] Psalm 103:12
[4] 2 Corinthians 5:21

ceased. Jesus became that one High Priest forever that the Levitical high priest had symbolised and pointed to for all those years. In the New Covenant, every believer is a priest with all of the same priestly responsibilities to intercede for the situations around them. It is now our responsibility to intercede for the situations brought to our attention, to bring Heaven into this earth.

And with a change of priesthood comes the change in sacrifice and change in location for that sacrifice. No longer is the Lord worshipped in a temple in Jerusalem, but in living temples[5] offering sacrifices of praise[6] and worship. Now that is some change! Next time you walk into a beautiful building built for the worship of the Lord, such as a magnificent medieval cathedral, then remember Jesus' words to His disciples on leaving the temple—a beautiful and wonderful building in its day—that there "shall not be left here one stone upon another, which shall not be thrown down," Mark 13:2. How much more precious, beautiful and valuable to Him is the worship from living temples.

Another key area that changed drastically from the Old Covenant to the New is the role and ministry of the Holy Spirit. Under the Old Covenant the Holy Spirit would come upon people for a specific purpose or season, until Jesus—for on Him, the Spirit stayed[7]. In the New Covenant one of the key markers has to be the infilling and indwelling of the Holy Spirit in the believer. So much results...from the inner transformation, and empowerment to break sinful and destructive old habits and ways, to the empowerment to release healing and deliverance to those around us and the situations we encounter. It is the

---

[5] 2 Corinthians 6:16
[6] Romans 12:1 and 1 Peter 2:5
[7] John 1:33

Spirit's work within us, and through us, to bring Heaven here to this earth.

Another area that is changed, and many people have completely missed, is the role of the prophetic ministry, and prophecy. Under the Old Covenant, the prophetic ministry was so often to bring warning and judgement. But remember Jesus Himself said He came not to judge but to bring life, and this is a powerful reminder and illustration of how the New Covenant prophetic ministry should operate. It is not hard to look at sin and declare judgement over it—that does not require faith. That is Old Covenant. Rather, we are called to see through the eyes of Faith what the Lord would bring in its place, and declare and release that. To look at someone locked and addicted to heroin and declare he is a righteous man of faith requires hearing and seeing something quite different. But this very declaration is what sets the person free to become that. Drawing out the gold and releasing someone's destiny is prophetic Grace indeed.

By way of illustration, it is easy to declare God's judgement and earthquakes and destruction over California. With the fault lines running through the state, such a declaration is hardly a declaration stemming from Faith. There is much sin to warrant judgement. However there is also a mighty moving of the Holy Spirit. Should we not rather be like Abraham interceding for Sodom, asking the Lord to withhold His judgement for the sake of the righteous there? Similarly, how few are the nations that stand by and publically support Israel. How many condemn her every move, thereby heaping judgement on themselves. So do we prophecy calamity and destruction and God's Judgement on those nations or do we declare His Grace and Covenant Assistance? Remember that we too are just as undeserving.

So Mercy, too, is also changed at the cross. From covenantally obligated assistance, we are now called to a life of offering assistance. This is obligated no longer by covenant, but by the need of our fellow man in the light of the assistance so freely lavished on us. And like sacrifice, Mercy costs, and is not easily given away. There is no guarantee of the recipient's response, as there can be no manipulation or ulterior motive with Mercy. Freely we have received, freely we give.[8]

Perhaps I should simply insert the whole of the Book of Hebrews at this point. But may I insert more than just a few key verses. The writer's starting point has to be to point people to Jesus, and illustrate His Glory from the Old Covenant, but for that I ask the reader to turn to it afresh in their favourite translation. I start here at Chapter 3.

> Old Covenant: Vs 5, And Moses verily was faithful in all his house, as a servant, for a testimony of those things which were to be spoken after
>
> New Covenant: Vs 6, But Christ as a son over his own house; whose house are we, if we hold fast the confidence and the rejoicing of the hope firm unto the end.
>
> Hebrews 4: Old Covenant: Vs 8, For if Jesus had given them rest, then would he not afterward have spoken of another day.
>
> New Covenant: Vs 9, There remaineth therefore a rest to the people of God...
>
> Vs 11, Let us labour therefore to enter into that rest, lest any man fall after the same example of unbelief.

---

[8] Matthew 10:8

No matter which translation you choose, they all still have that wonderful contradiction, that we have 'work' to do, to enter our New Covenant 'rest'.

See how the Levitical High Priest has now been made obsolete by a very different High Priest? Jesus didn't come from the tribe of Levi, so He had no right to be a priest under the Old Covenant. But here the writer explains His priesthood was after the order of Melchisedec, and not Aaron at all. Evidently this is of a higher order than the Levitical priesthood. Melchisedec was the priest to whom Abraham gave the tithe of his takings from his battle, when he went to rescue Lot. Melchisedec had no lineage, so was a very strange person indeed, but whose titles were King of Salem, and King of Peace. For the detail refer to Genesis 14:8.

Now, the writer to the Hebrews hadn't dreamed this himself, but was only quoting Psalm 110:4. Remember Jesus Himself quoted this at the religious leaders in Matthew 22: 43-45. But not only was Jesus a priest from a higher order than Aaron, He was a hugely better high priest.

> Hebrews 4:14-16 Seeing then that we have a great high priest, that is passed into the heavens, Jesus the Son of God, let us hold fast our profession. For we have not an high priest which cannot be touched with the feeling of our infirmities; but was in all points tempted like as we are, yet without sin. Let us therefore come boldly unto the throne of grace, that we may obtain mercy, and find grace to help in time of need.

Let us remember He said He didn't come into the world to judge it, but to give us life.[9] And even when thrown into the

---

[9] John 3:17

position of judge, as with the woman caught in adultery, He said to her, "Neither do I condemn you. Go and sin no more."[10] What a high priest we have! Let us indeed come boldly to the throne of grace... He is saying to you and me, "I haven't come to judge you, but to give you life."

> Hebrews 5:1-10 For every high priest taken from among men is ordained for men in things pertaining to God, that he may offer both gifts and sacrifices for sins: who can have compassion on the ignorant, and on them that are out of the way; for that he himself also is compassed with infirmity. And by reason hereof he ought, as for the people, so also for himself, to offer for sins. And no man taketh this honour unto himself, but he that is called of God, as was Aaron. So also Christ glorified not himself to be made an high priest; but he that said unto him, Thou art my Son, to day have I begotten thee. As he saith also in another place, Thou art a priest for ever after the order of Melchisedec. Who in the days of his flesh, when he had offered up prayers and supplications with strong crying and tears unto him that was able to save him from death, and was heard in that he feared; though he were a Son, yet learned he obedience by the things which he suffered; and being made perfect, he became the author of eternal salvation unto all them that obey him; called of God an high priest after the order of Melchisedec.

---

[10] John 8:11

Hebrews 6: Old Covenant: Vs 13-15 For when God made promise to Abraham, because he could swear by no greater, he sware by himself, saying, Surely blessing I will bless thee, and multiplying I will multiply thee. And so, after he had patiently endured, he obtained the promise.

New Covenant: Vs 16-20 For men verily swear by the greater: and an oath for confirmation is to them an end of all strife. Wherein God, willing more abundantly to shew unto the heirs of promise the immutability of his counsel, confirmed it by an oath: that by two immutable things, in which it was impossible for God to lie, we might have a strong consolation, who have fled for refuge to lay hold upon the hope set before us: which hope we have as an anchor of the soul, both sure and steadfast, and which entereth into that within the veil; whither the forerunner is for us entered, even Jesus, made an high priest for ever after the order of Melchisedec.

So God is here bending over backwards to convey the certainty of His help and assistance, to us New Covenant heirs of all He has promised. He doesn't need to promise and then swear. He does this entirely for our benefit, that we may "lay hold of the hope set before us." Faith being the assurance of things hoped for.[11] Hope is the seed from which faith can grow; the foundation upon which faith can build, "an anchor for the soul".

What an anchor! Sure and steadfast. The 'veil' referred to here is the thick curtain that separated the Holy of Holies, that

---

[11] Hebrews 11:1

central focus where God was present, from the outer court of the temple, where the people could gather. It was through this veil that the High Priest entered to present the blood of atonement. But now, under our New Covenant, it is you and I who are called to enter that most holy of places in the heavenly realms, following in Jesus footsteps. Remember that the veil of the temple was torn in two at Jesus' death—'from the top to the bottom.'[12]

> Hebrews 7:17-18 For it is declared: "You are a priest forever, in the order of Melchizedek." The former regulation is set aside because it was weak and useless (for the law made nothing perfect), and a better hope is introduced, by which we draw near to God. (NIV)

While exploring the reality of Jesus being a high priest, while not being born from the appropriate tribe, the writer slips in this wonderful statement; the former regulation of the Old Covenant has been set aside. It could never make anyone perfect—ah-ha, but our New Covenant DOES make people perfect—yes, YOU, and even Me. Now that's a better hope. We do not have to wait until we die to be made perfect—or the spirit of death would have that glory.

> Hebrews 7:20-25 And it was not without an oath. Others became priests without any oath, but he became a priest with an oath when God said to him: "The Lord has sworn and will not change his mind: 'You are a priest forever.'" Because of this oath, *Jesus has become the guarantor of a better covenant.* Now there have been many of those priests, since death prevented them from

---

[12] Matthew 27:51

continuing in office; but because Jesus lives forever, he has a permanent priesthood. ***Therefore he is able to save completely those who come to God through him, because he always lives to*** intercede ***for them.*** (NIV)(emphasis mine)

Our salvation is not a half measure or a whitewash that looks nice on the outside. No one is beyond its reach and beyond its ability to completely transform, but we do have to come to God through Him. No one can do that for us—we have to do that for ourselves; we each have to respond to His offer. God has no grandchildren.

> Hebrews 7:26-28 Such a high priest truly meets our need—one who is holy, blameless, pure, set apart from sinners, exalted above the heavens. Unlike the other high priests, he does not need to offer sacrifices day after day, first for his own sins, and then for the sins of the people. He sacrificed for their sins once for all when he offered himself. For the law appoints as high priests men in all their weakness; but the oath, which came after the law, appointed the Son, who has been made perfect forever. (NIV)

Hebrews 8: The High Priest of a New Covenant

> Vs 1-2 Now the main point of what we are saying is this: We do have such a high priest, who sat down at the right hand of the throne of the Majesty in heaven, and who serves in the sanctuary, the true tabernacle set up by the Lord, not by a mere human being. (NIV)

So all of the previous paragraphs have been leading to this point—the wonder of having Jesus as our forever perfect high priest always interceding on our behalf at the Father's right hand—now that's close. Do you wonder in those dark times, whether there is anyone pleading your case with Father; does anyone hear your desperate cry for assistance? Rest assured, Jesus has been there before you and He is representing you like no other.

> Hebrews 8:3-6 Every high priest is appointed to offer both gifts and sacrifices, and so it was necessary for this one also to have something to offer. If he were on earth, he would not be a priest, for there are already priests who offer the gifts prescribed by the law. They serve at a sanctuary that is a copy and shadow of what is in heaven. This is why Moses was warned when he was about to build the tabernacle: "See to it that you make everything according to the pattern shown you on the mountain." But in fact the ***ministry Jesus has received is as superior to theirs as the covenant of which he is mediator is superior to the old one, since the new covenant is established on better promises***. (NIV) (emphasis mine)

Our New Covenant is so much better than the Old! It achieves so much more, and it is founded on so much better promises. But notice the incredible similarities running through them, in that they are both binding blood covenant agreements.

> Vs 7-13, For if there had been nothing wrong with that first covenant, no place would have been sought for another. But God found fault with the people and said: ***"The days are coming, declares***

the Lord, when I will make a new covenant with the people of Israel and with the people of Judah. It will not be like the covenant I made with their ancestors when I took them by the hand to lead them out of Egypt, because they did not remain faithful to my covenant, and I turned away from them, declares the Lord.

This is the covenant I will establish with the people of Israel after that time, declares the Lord. *I will put my laws in their minds and write them on their hearts. I will be their God, and they will be my people.* No longer will they teach their neighbour, or say to one another, 'Know the Lord,' because they will all know me, from the least of them to the greatest.

For I will forgive their wickedness and will remember their sins no more." *By calling this covenant "new," he has made the first one obsolete; and what is obsolete* and outdated will soon disappear. (NIV) (emphasis mine)

Look at the theological problems the early church had in freeing itself from the Old Covenant Law and legalism. Peter, Barnabas, and many others were chastised by Paul in no uncertain terms because they had not got that clear distinction down into their thinking in the way Paul—that Pharisee of Pharisees—had. The old Law is now completely obsolete and sure enough, the temple that stood at the centre of the Law was about to disappear. The temple of the New Covenant is not made of stone but is the hearts of us New Covenant believers, where the Holy Spirit takes up residence.

Keeping all of those Old Covenant rules and regulations had not made them perfect, or brought them closer to God. It had highlighted their sin and their need for a Saviour. Paul had to remind them that their right standing before God, was through faith in Jesus, and only through faith in Jesus, whether they were Jew or Gentile. See Galatians 2:11-16.

> Hebrews 9:11-14 But when Christ came as high priest of the good things that are now already here, he went through the greater and more perfect tabernacle that is not made with human hands, that is to say, is not a part of this creation. He did not enter by means of the blood of goats and calves; but he entered the Most Holy Place once for all by his own blood, thus obtaining eternal redemption. The blood of goats and bulls and the ashes of a heifer sprinkled on those who are ceremonially unclean sanctify them so that they are outwardly clean. How much more, then, will the blood of Christ, who through the eternal Spirit offered himself unblemished to God, cleanse our consciences from acts that lead to death, so that we may serve the living God. (NIV) (emphasis mine)

How much more—oh, how much more.... will the blood of Christ cleanse our conscience so that we may serve the Living God. Oh Yes, Yes, Yes, and Amen!

> Vs 15-28, For this reason Christ is the guarantor of a new covenant, that those who are called may receive the promised eternal inheritance—now that he has died as a ransom to set them free from the sins committed under the first covenant.
>
> In the case of a will, it is necessary to prove the death of the one who made it, because a will is in force only when somebody has died; it never takes

124

effect while the one who made it is living. This is why even the first covenant was not put into effect without blood. When Moses had proclaimed every command of the law to all the people, he took the blood of calves, together with water, scarlet wool and branches of hyssop, and sprinkled the scroll and all the people. He said, "This is the blood of the covenant, which God has commanded you to keep." In the same way, he sprinkled with the blood both the tabernacle and everything used in its ceremonies. In fact, the law requires that nearly everything be cleansed with blood, and without the shedding of blood there is no forgiveness.

It was necessary, then, for the copies of the heavenly things to be purified with these sacrifices, but the heavenly things themselves with better sacrifices than these. For Christ did not enter a sanctuary made with human hands that was only a copy of the true one; he entered heaven itself, now to appear for us in God's presence. Nor did he enter heaven to offer himself again and again, the way the high priest enters the Most Holy Place every year with blood that is not his own. Otherwise Christ would have had to suffer many times since the creation of the world. But he has appeared once for all at the culmination of the ages to do away with sin by the sacrifice of himself. Just as people are destined to die once, and after that to face judgment, so Christ was sacrificed once to take away the sins of many; and he will appear a second time, not to bear sin, but to bring salvation to those who are waiting for him. (emphasis mine)

> Hebrews 10:1 The law is only a shadow of the good things that are coming—not the realities themselves. For this reason it can never, by the same sacrifices repeated endlessly year after year, make perfect those who draw near to worship. (NIV)

Perhaps I should have simply inserted this one single verse. Oh please stop and read it again.

"The Old Covenant can never make perfect those who draw near to worship…"

So what does this say about the New Covenant that replaces it?

> Hebrews 10:2-10 Otherwise, would they not have stopped being offered? For the worshipers would have been cleansed once for all, and would no longer have felt guilty for their sins. 3 But those sacrifices are an annual reminder of sins. It is impossible for the blood of bulls and goats to take away sins.
>
> Therefore, when Christ came into the world, he said: "Sacrifice and offering you did not desire, but a body you prepared for me; with burnt offerings and sin offerings you were not pleased.
>
> Then I said, 'Here I am—it is written about me in the scroll—I have come to do your will, my God.'" First he said, "Sacrifices and offerings, burnt offerings and sin offerings you did not desire, nor were you pleased with them"—though they were offered in accordance with the law. Then he said, "Here I am, I have come to do your will." He sets aside the first to establish the second. And by that

will, we have been made holy through the sacrifice of the body of Jesus Christ once for all.

Jesus has set aside the Old Covenant and effectively cut and established a New Covenant, and the key achievement of this New Covenant is that it makes you and me holy and righteous. "He sets aside the Old to establish the New." All that was pointed to and promised in the Old Covenant is fulfilled and delivered by the New one.

> Vs 11-14, Day after day every priest stands and performs his religious duties; again and again he offers the same sacrifices, which can never take away sins. But when this priest had offered for all time one sacrifice for sins, he sat down at the right hand of God, and since that time he waits for his enemies to be made his footstool. For by one sacrifice he has made perfect forever those who are being made holy. (emphasis mine)

So here, quite definitively, you are pronounced perfect, through the shed blood of Jesus. So whether you feel perfect, whether it looks that way, or whatever, He declares that's what you are, while you are in the process of being made holy... Does your religion or your church continue to remind you of your sin and imperfection? Then religion is what it is, and not New Covenant Christianity.

> Vs 15-17, The Holy Spirit also testifies to us about this. First he says: "This is the covenant I will make with them after that time, says the Lord. I will put my laws in their hearts, and I will write them on their minds." Then he adds: "Their sins and lawless acts I will remember no more." (NIV)

Our sin is not forgotten, it is blotted out. If it was forgotten, then maybe it would one day be remembered. All record of it is blotted out, and God Himself 'chooses' to remember it no more [13.] [14, 15] Now if God Himself chooses to remember it no more, then I think we probably need to take a leaf out of his book, and do much the same. Do you forever confess your sin before Him? Do you go over and over confessing what He has chosen to remember no more?

> Vs 18, And where these have been forgiven, sacrifice for sin is no longer necessary. (NIV)

Amazing!

Think through this for a minute. Is this your experience? That ALL of your sin has been forgiven and blotted out? All trace of it, and its potential hold on you has been wiped away.

I love the increasing number of testimonies of those who self-harmed and bear the scars, until one day not only was their heart wiped clean, and their memory healed, but even the physical scars are erased by their Heavenly Daddy.

The moment you and I confessed it, it was blotted out, never to be remembered again. So even if you walk out and do the same thing again, for Him it is the first time.

You and I are **not** sinners saved by grace.

Once we have taken Jesus as our Lord and Saviour, we are children and friends of the Most High. We are clothed with His Righteousness. We are the very Righteousness of God, in Christ Jesus.[16] Most of us are well rehearsed in seeing ourselves as sinners, and living that way. But that is not the truth for a New Covenant believer. We need to be practising a very different

---

[13] Jeremiah 31:34
[14] Hebrews 8:12
[15] Hebrews 10:17
[16] 2 Corinthians 5:21

mindset. What does it mean to be a priest like Jesus, with immediate and ready access to God? Are you well-rehearsed in this?

A Call to Persevere in Faith

> Hebrews 11:19-22 Therefore, brothers and sisters, since we have confidence to enter the Most Holy Place by the blood of Jesus, by a new and living way opened for us through the curtain, that is, his body, and since we have a great priest over the house of God, let us draw near to God with a sincere heart and with the full assurance that faith brings, having our hearts sprinkled to cleanse us from a guilty conscience and having our bodies washed with pure water.

So the way is open for us to enter with confidence the Most Holy Place through the blood of Jesus. Do we avail ourselves of this amazing and wonderful invitation? This is an invitation to draw on His mercy—His covenant assistance. Do you or the world around you need this help? I and my world most definitely do.

> Vs 23-25, Let us hold unswervingly to the hope we profess, for he who promised is faithful. And let us consider how we may spur one another on toward love and good deeds, not giving up meeting together, as some are in the habit of doing, but encouraging one another—and all the more as you see the Day approaching. (NIV)

Maybe this chapter is too long already, but I want to spur you on and spur you on again.

Hebrews 12:1-4 Wherefore seeing we also are compassed about with so great a cloud of witnesses, let us lay aside every weight, and the sin which doth so easily beset us, and let us run with patience the race that is set before us. Looking unto Jesus the author and finisher of our faith; who for the joy that was set before him endured the cross, despising the shame, and is set down at the right hand of the throne of God. For consider him that endured such contradiction of sinners against himself, lest ye be wearied and faint in your minds. Ye have not yet resisted unto blood, striving against sin.

Is there anywhere such a call as this? Let us run this race, and cast aside whatever trips us up. And what an example we have in our King Jesus.

Hebrews 12:18 Old Covenant: For ye are not come unto the mount that might be touched, and that burned with fire, nor unto blackness, and darkness, and tempest,

New Covenant: Vs 22-24 But ye are come unto mount Zion, and unto the city of the living God, the heavenly Jerusalem, and to an innumerable company of angels, to the general assembly and church of the firstborn, which are written in heaven, and to God the Judge of all, and to the spirits of just men made perfect, and to Jesus the mediator of the new covenant, and to the blood of sprinkling, that speaketh better things than that of Abel.

From the pressures of life and other people, what flows

from your heart and your reactions? What exudes from your life and mine? Is it righteous vengeance, like Abel, whose blood cried out from the ground,[17] or is it MERCY and forgiveness like Jesus?[18] Oh that's a tough one. Let us indeed come to Jesus and be so full of His Spirit that Mercy seeps from the pores of every part of us.

> Here's our New Covenant sacrifice: Hebrews 13:15 By him therefore let us offer the sacrifice of praise to God continually, that is, the fruit of our lips giving thanks to his name…
>
> Hebrews 13:20-21 Now the God of peace, that brought again from the dead our Lord Jesus, that great shepherd of the sheep, through the blood of the everlasting covenant, Make you perfect in every good work to do his will, working in you that which is well pleasing in his sight, through Jesus Christ; to whom be glory for ever and ever. Amen.

The writer to the Hebrews was writing to a people with a covenantal view of their God. We too need to come back to this same mindset; to this same framework, to this same understanding of who God is and how He wants us to see and relate to Him. He longs for us to come with simple confidence to His throne of grace to request and walk away with all that we and those around us need, "according to His riches in Glory."

Remember that fateful night Jesus began by washing the disciples' feet. This covenant is not just for us, but rather that through us, Father's blessing, healing, restoration and gifts would flow through us, as we serve those around us with His servant mindset.

---

[17] Genesis 4:10
[18] Luke 23:34

Conclusion

Let us remember Jesus as He requested we do.

This covenant makes perfect those who draw near to worship.

So let us avail ourselves of what is so freely offered to us; let us honour Jesus and **Press in** to what He paid such a price for, on our behalf. We owe it to Him.

Is every area of your life abounding in health, wholeness and prosperity—your health, your family, your bank balance, your job, your dreams and your heart abounding in Hope? These perhaps are easy to list, but how is your relationship with Papa God, with Jesus and Holy Spirit?

Come boldly to the throne of Grace to find the help, and covenant assistance for yourself and those around you in need.

Our fellowship with Father, Son and Holy Spirit is hugely precious and so easily derailed by plenty. Keep the channel of love flowing from Heaven to earth with your open heart and generous lifestyle.

Part 7: The Old Covenants

Chapter 19
The Patriarchal Covenants

In order for there to be a New Covenant—which is key—there must have been an "Old" Covenant to be replaced. So to learn many of the aspects worthy of our attention in the New Covenant, it is essential that we also examine the Old. But even before the Old Covenant was set up, God had already made covenants with the Patriarchs, Abraham, Isaac and Jacob. These, curiously, are much closer to our New Covenant, and well worthy of study.

The Patriarchal Covenants share most of the common features of covenant as I have outlined in our look at the very nature and heart of "covenant":

A definitive point of agreement (or a number of points)
Defined participants
Defined Blessings (and cursings in some places)
Conditions
An inauguration ceremony
Setting up the Memorial
A celebratory meal

A look through the life of Abraham reveals the Lord spoke to him and made promises to him on various occasions, such as Genesis 12:

Vs 1-3, Leave your country, your people and your father's household and go to the land I will show you. "I will make you into a great nation and I will bless you; I will make your name great, and you will be a blessing. I will bless those who bless you, and whoever curses you I will curse; and all peoples on earth will be blessed through you."

This is simply a nice promise (okay, a **very** nice promise.), but we do not get a covenant description, until we get to Genesis chapter 15, and here we have a full-bloodied description of a blood covenant drawn up and "cut" between Abram and God:

> Genesis 15:9-21 So the LORD said to him, "Bring me a heifer, a goat and a ram, each three years old, along with a dove and a young pigeon." Abram brought all these to him, cut them in two and arranged the halves opposite each other; the birds, however, he did not cut in half. Then birds of prey came down on the carcasses, but Abram drove them away. As the sun was setting, Abram fell into a deep sleep, and a thick and dreadful darkness came over him.
>
> Then the LORD said to him, "Know for certain that your descendants will be strangers in a country not their own, and they will be enslaved and mistreated four hundred years. But I will punish the nation they serve as slaves, and afterward they will come out with great possessions. You, however, will go to your fathers in peace and be buried at a good old age. In the fourth generation your descendants will come back here, for the sin of the Amorites has not yet reached its full measure."

When the sun had set and darkness had fallen, a smoking firepot with a blazing torch appeared and passed between the pieces. On that day the LORD made a covenant with Abram and said, "To your descendants I give this land, from the river of Egypt to the great river, the Euphrates—the land of the Kenites, Kenizzites, Kadmonites, Hittites, Perizzites, Rephaites, Amorites, Canaanites, Girgashites and Jebusites." (NIV)

Interesting in this description is that there are no conditions on Abram's part. Normally both parties would walk between the two halves laid out on the ground, but in this instance God Himself—alone walks through. This is renewed in Genesis 17, but now extended to be an everlasting covenant, but with the condition that they keep circumcision.

Genesis 17:1-14 When Abram was ninety-nine years old, the LORD appeared to him and said, "I am God Almighty; walk before me and be blameless. will confirm my covenant between me and you and will greatly increase your numbers."

Abram fell facedown, and God said to him, "As for me, this is my covenant with you: You will be the father of many nations. No longer will you be called Abram; your name will be Abraham, for I have made you a father of many nations. I will make you very fruitful; I will make nations of you, and kings will come from you. I will establish my covenant as an everlasting covenant between me and you and your descendants after you for the generations to come, to be your God and the God of your descendants after you. The whole land of Canaan, where you are now an alien, I will give as an everlasting possession to you and your descendants after you; and I will be their God."

Then God said to Abraham, "As for you, you must keep my covenant, you and your descendants after you for the generations to come. This is my covenant with you and your descendants after you, the covenant you are to keep: Every male among you shall be circumcised. You are to undergo circumcision, and it will be the sign of the covenant between me and you. For the generations to come every male among you who is eight days old must be circumcised, including those born in your household or bought with money from a foreigner—those who are not your offspring. Whether born in your household or bought with your money, they must be circumcised. My covenant in your flesh is to be an everlasting covenant. Any uncircumcised male, who has not been circumcised in the flesh, will be cut off from his people; he has broken my covenant." (NIV)

In the light of his circumstances Abram was having a hard time with this. (I think we would have too.)

Vs 15-22, God also said to Abraham, "As for Sarai your wife, you are no longer to call her Sarai; her name will be Sarah. I will bless her and will surely give you a son by her. I will bless her so that she will be the mother of nations; kings of peoples will come from her." Abraham fell facedown; he laughed and said to himself, "Will a son be born to a man a hundred years old? Will Sarah bear a child at the age of ninety?" And Abraham said to God, "If only Ishmael might live under your blessing."

136

Then God said, "Yes, but your wife Sarah will bear you a son, and you will call him Isaac I will establish my covenant with him as an everlasting covenant for his descendants after him. But my covenant I will establish with Isaac, whom Sarah will bear to you by this time next year." When he had finished speaking with Abraham, God went up from him.

Genesis does not tell us the time interval between chapters 17, and 18, except it can't have been more than three months as God promises Abraham a son "by this time next year", and Sarah clearly is still not pregnant in chapter 18. She is still far from believing she will be—see chapter 18:12. But Isaac is born when Abraham is 100—so in the timeframe promised; see chapter 21:2 and 5.

This may well sound all wonderful and theoretical, but for a number of things that we so easily skip over. Firstly the Lord Himself appears to Abram/Abraham in chapters 17 and 18. Abraham clearly recognized the Lord at the beginning of chapter 18. Secondly the nature of covenant was clearly understood and established by Abraham.

We see him enacting a covenant with Abimilech: In Genesis 21:22-32, And it came to pass at that time, that Abimelech and Phichol the chief captain of his host spake unto Abraham, saying, God is with thee in all that thou doest: now therefore swear unto me here by God that thou wilt not deal falsely with me, nor with my son, nor with my son's son: but according to the kindness that I have done unto thee, thou shalt do unto me, and to the land wherein thou hast sojourned.

And Abraham said, I will swear. And Abraham reproved Abimelech because of a well of water, which Abimelech's servants had violently taken away. And Abimelech said, "I wot not who hath done this thing; neither didst thou tell me, neither yet heard I of it, but to day." And Abraham took sheep and oxen, and gave them unto Abimelech; and both of them made a covenant. And Abraham set seven ewe lambs of the flock by themselves.

And Abimelech said unto Abraham, "What mean these seven ewe lambs which thou hast set by themselves?"

And he said, "For these seven ewe lambs shalt thou take of my hand, that they may be a witness unto me, that I have digged this well."

Wherefore he called that place Beersheba; because there they sware both of them.

Thus they made a covenant at Beersheba: then Abimelech rose up, and Phichol the chief captain of his host, and they returned into the land of the Philistines. (NIV)

Not spelled out as a covenant, but we find the Lord appearing to Isaac in very similar fashion to his appearing to Abraham:

Genesis 26:1-5 And there was a famine in the land, beside the first famine that was in the days of Abraham. And Isaac went unto Abimelech king of the Philistines unto Gerar. And the LORD appeared unto him, and said, Go not down into

Egypt; dwell in the land which I shall tell thee of: sojourn in this land, and I will be with thee, and will bless thee; for unto thee, and unto thy seed, I will give all these countries, and I will perform the oath which I sware unto Abraham thy father; and I will make thy seed to multiply as the stars of heaven, and will give unto thy seed all these countries; and in thy seed shall all the nations of the earth be blessed; because that Abraham obeyed my voice, and kept my charge, my commandments, my statutes, and my laws.

Now Isaac reaped a hundredfold in that famine—verse 12—and ended up with his enemies coming to him to cut covenant with him for their own protection, because "We saw plainly that Jehovah was with thee," verse 28. So it is tempting to think the harvest just materialised out of thin air. Of course nothing could be further from the truth—Isaac's servants were busy digging wells for irrigating the crops while Abimilech's and Phicol's were busy filling the wells in, or trying to pinch the wells that Isaac's servants had been busy digging. It looks as though this famine was very man-made.

Remember the Lord promises to "bless all the work of your hands"…so they need to be doing something blessable.

And similarly the Lord appears to Jacob in a dream, in his flight in fear from Esau:

Genesis 28:12-22 And he dreamed, and behold a ladder set up on the earth, and the top of it reached to heaven: and behold the angels of God ascending and descending on it. And, behold, the LORD stood above it, and said, "I am the LORD God of Abraham thy father, and the God of Isaac: the land whereon thou liest, to thee will I give it, and to thy seed; and thy seed shall be as the dust of the earth, and thou shalt spread abroad to the west, and to the east, and to the north, and to the south: and in thee and in thy seed shall all the families of the earth be blessed. And, behold, I am with thee, and will keep thee in all places whither thou goest, and will bring thee again into this land; for I will not leave thee, until I have done that which I have spoken to thee of."

And Jacob awaked out of his sleep, and he said, Surely the LORD is in this place; and I knew it not. And he was afraid, and said, How dreadful is this place. This is none other but the house of God, and this is the gate of heaven. And Jacob rose up early in the morning, and took the stone that he had put for his pillows, and set it up for a pillar, and poured oil upon the top of it. And he called the name of that place Bethel: but the name of that city was called Luz at the first. And Jacob vowed a vow, saying, "If God will be with me, and will keep me in this way that I go, and will give me bread to eat, and raiment to put on, so that I come again to my father's house in peace; then shall the LORD be my God: and this stone, which I have set for a pillar, shall be God's house: and of all that thou shalt give me I will surely give the tenth unto thee."

Conclusion

Our Heavenly Father's covenant promises to us are outrageous. If they don't cause you to roll up with laughter at their sheer impossibility, then maybe you haven't quite been listening.

Yes, His promises to you and to me are that crazy. So when Jesus returns, will He find faith on the earth? (Luke 18:8) Will He find people crazy enough to laugh, but then believe Him and take Him at His word?

Chapter 20

Understanding the Old Patriarchal Covenants

I wondered just how much Abraham actually understood of the Covenant he had with the Lord—that was, until I read on to Genesis chapter 22 and the offering of Isaac—the Child of Promise, in the context of Covenant. This makes absolutely no sense without an understanding of Covenant—and clearly writers and theologians through the ages have had a hard time with it. The Lord has never asked anyone to sacrifice his child to Him—it has always been completely abhorrent to those who have any understanding of Him and His ways.

But in the light of Blood Covenant—this makes perfect sense. A Blood Covenant includes the essential ingredient of reciprocity. Anything I require of you—you will do, *and in exchange*, anything you require of me I will do….

Now Abraham knew he needed a Redeemer—a Saviour—in order to have a relationship with the Righteous God. As we so well understand from our New Covenant perspective, this Saviour has to be perfect—to be sinless, nothing less will do. So Abraham takes Isaac to the altar of sacrifice, effectively saying to God Almighty, "I know you have a Son; are you prepared to offer Him as that perfect sacrifice for me? I'm prepared to offer my son to you—inadequate though that is. Isaac is the fulfilment of Your promise to me—he is the 'child of promise' with all that that means." But by this act Abraham is "obligating God" to send His Son Jesus to be this sacrifice for himself and all of us too—on the basis of covenantal reciprocity.

No wonder when Isaac asks, "Where's the lamb for the sacrifice?" Abraham responds with, "God Himself will provide." This is the very heart—the reason—for the whole encounter.

It was not lost on Isaac either, for in the next few chapters we see that the Lord appears to Isaac on a number of occasions as He had to Abraham—Genesis 26:2 is an example. Just who this person is, who had met and talked with his father, Isaac well understands. Of all of them, Isaac would be dead meat were it not for His Redeemer. He is also well recognised by Jacob, Isaac's son, where He is translated as "The Redeeming Angel", as he sums up his life in blessing the sons of Joseph:

> Genesis 48:15-16 May the God before whom my fathers Abraham and Isaac walked, the God who has been my shepherd all my life to this day, the Redeeming Angel who has delivered me from all harm—may he bless these boys. (NIV) (emphasis mine)

Not such a bad description of Jesus appearing ahead of time.

I'm always amused by Jesus retort to the Jews, recounted in John 8:56-58

> Your father Abraham rejoiced to see my day: and he saw it, and was glad. Then said the Jews unto him, Thou art not yet fifty years old, and hast thou seen Abraham? Jesus said unto them, Verily, verily, I say unto you, Before Abraham was, I am.

Did those patriarchs understand and relate to God as we do? I rather think they knew Jesus—their Redeemer—better than we do. They met Him, they recognized Him, they invited Him into their tents and sat and cooked Him a meal. He made outrageous promises to them, that made them laugh at their absurdity—and He fulfilled them to the letter.

Did they understand what it was to have a covenant with the Almighty One? I rather think they understood this a whole lot more than we do. They knew this covenant was based on their Redeemer fulfilling the sacrifice on their behalf. All they had to do was to circumcise the males in the family and see Him guard, guide and enrich their lives beyond their wildest dreams. And yes—they freely acknowledged they owed it all to Him. Look afresh at Jacob's summation of His life, "*the God who has been my shepherd all my life to this day,* the Redeeming Angel who has delivered me from all harm....." There are few contemporary believers who could sum up their Lord and their life so simply or so succinctly.

But one deep fundamental question remains to be answered. Why on earth should a God whose very word is "Yes and Amen" choose to cut covenant with man?

I'm so glad it doesn't fall to me to try and answer that so-obvious question. As I concluded in the introduction, fortunately, the writer of the Book of Hebrews settles this one for us:

> Hebrews 6:13-20 When God made his promise to Abraham, since there was no one greater for him to swear by, he swore by himself, saying, "I will surely bless you and give you many descendants." And so after waiting patiently, Abraham received what was promised.

> People swear by someone greater than themselves, and the oath confirms what is said and puts an end to all argument. Because God wanted to make the unchanging nature of his purpose very clear to the heirs of what was promised, he confirmed it with an oath. God did this so that, by two unchangeable things in which it is impossible for God to lie, we

who have fled to take hold of the hope set before us **may be greatly encouraged**. We have this hope as an anchor for the soul, firm and secure. It enters the inner sanctuary behind the curtain, where our forerunner, Jesus, has entered on our behalf. He has become a high priest forever, in the order of Melchizedek. (NIV) (emphasis mine)

Conclusion

The Lord desperately wanted the Patriarchs to be in absolutely NO DOUBT as to His desire to bless them beyond their wildest imaginations!

Does He want anything less for His New Covenant partners?

Chapter 21
Introduction to the Mosaic Covenant

The Mosaic Covenant is quite different to the Covenants made with the Patriarchs, but obviously has all the same "covenantal" ingredients. Much more specifically spelled out in the Mosaic Covenant are the terms necessary to fulfil the human side of this agreement. (Unfortunately, terms that no man could possibly fulfil—except Jesus.)

The Mosaic Covenant shares all of the common features of Covenant as we have outlined in our look at the very nature and heart of "covenant":

A definitive point of agreement (in this case a number of points)

Defined participants

Defined Blessings (and cursings in some places)

Conditions

An inauguration ceremony with the shedding of blood

Setting up the Memorial

A celebratory meal

So great blessings are spelled out, side by side with the corresponding curses, in typical covenant fashion, as in Deuteronomy 28…

But the Holy Spirit is a master at pulling many threads together in parallel. At one level He is spelling out a Covenant with its terms and conditions. But in so doing He is also spelling out a Covenant that Jesus will one day fulfil to the letter so that we all reap the benefit under the New Covenant.

But not content with this He is also spelling out all of the details of sacrifice and worship that mirror, copy, symbolize and typify, or parallel their real fulfilment by Jesus. So the sacrificial offering of the Covenant is an exact portrayal, and re-enactment using a lamb, of what was going to happen to Jesus thousands of years later.

But at yet another level, too, what is also spelled out is a parallel of what will happen in the Heavenlies. This is almost incomprehensible to me—that lucifer's fall corrupted something in Heavenly Places. Very little of Jesus' Blood trickled out onto the earth at Calvary. We have looked at the trail of that Blood and all that is covered by it. As the writer of Hebrews puts it of the earthly priests, that they "serve at a sanctuary that is a copy and shadow of what is in heaven." So rising from the tomb, Jesus ascends to Heaven, to serve in the heavenlies. This is why Moses was warned when he was about to build the tabernacle: "See to it that you make everything according to the pattern shown you on the mountain," Hebrews 8:5; 8:6: "But the ministry Jesus has received is as superior to theirs as the covenant of which he is mediator is superior to the old one, and it is founded on better promises."

> Hebrews 9:11-15 When Christ came as high priest of the good things that are already here, he went through the greater and more perfect tabernacle that is not man-made, that is to say, not a part of this creation. He did not enter by means of the blood of goats and calves; *but he entered the Most Holy Place once for all by his own blood, having obtained eternal redemption.* The blood of goats and bulls and the ashes of a heifer sprinkled on those who are ceremonially unclean sanctify them so that they are outwardly clean. How much more, then, will the blood of Christ, who through the eternal Spirit offered himself unblemished to God, cleanse our consciences from acts that lead to

death, so that we may serve the living God. For this reason Christ is the mediator of a new covenant, that those who are called may receive the promised eternal inheritance—now that he has died as a ransom to set them free from the sins committed under the first covenant. (NIV) (emphasis mine)

That the true Mercy Seat is in Heavenly places, and Jesus' Blood had to be poured out there, I have no problem with. But the writer to the Hebrews goes on…

Adding yet further, and more specifically:

Hebrews 9:23-28 "It was necessary, then, for the copies of the heavenly things to be purified with these sacrifices, but the heavenly things themselves with better sacrifices than these. For Christ did not enter a man-made sanctuary that was only a copy of the true one; he entered heaven itself, now to appear for us in God's presence. Nor did he enter heaven to offer himself again and again, the way the high priest enters the Most Holy Place every year with blood that is not his own. Then Christ would have had to suffer many times since the creation of the world. But now he has appeared once for all at the end of the ages to do away with sin by the sacrifice of himself. Just as man is destined to die once, and after that to face judgment, so Christ was sacrificed once to take away the sins of many people; and he will appear a second time, not to bear sin, but to bring salvation to those who are waiting for him. (italics mine) (NIV)

So things in Heaven also needed to be cleansed by His blood—once and for all. No wonder then that he says to Mary in the garden in the first light of that resurrection Sunday, "Don't touch me. I have not yet ascended to my Father." All heaven is awaiting His entrance, to present His blood on the Heavenly altar. And then see how Jesus describes himself to His disciples that same evening, Luke 24:39, "Look at my hands and my feet. It is I myself! Touch me and see; a ghost does not have flesh and bones, as you see I have." (NIV)

He does not say as we would, "Flesh and blood," but flesh and bone. His blood has indeed been poured out on the heavenly altar, and his arteries are now filled with the Glory of the throne room—the true Holy of Holies—which the Mercy Seat simply illustrated.

Conclusion

What a covenant. What a promise. What a Saviour!

Remember, we are here talking about an All MIGHTY GOD making an unbelievably binding promise with the likes of you and I. Amazing!

It cost HIM His only Son; His and Holy Spirit's closest and most precious and intimate relationship.

The price is fully paid. The covenant has been cut. All is done—for us to freely enter.

Chapter 22
Cutting The Mosaic Covenant

Exodus 19:4-6 You yourselves have seen what I did to Egypt, and how I carried you on eagles' wings and brought you to myself. Now if you obey me fully and keep my covenant, then out of all nations you will be my treasured possession. Although the whole earth is mine, you will be for me a kingdom of priests and a holy nation. (NIV)

So the Lord's intention is for a kingdom of priests—and a Holy nation.

Next, He gives them the Ten Commandments—as obedience was a key part of the contract—and this was what He required obedience to.

Exodus 20:1-17 And God spoke all these words: "I am the LORD your God, who brought you out of Egypt, out of the land of slavery. "You shall have no other gods before me.

"You shall not make for yourself an image in the form of anything in heaven above or on the earth beneath or in the waters below. You shall not bow down to them or worship them; for I, the LORD your God, am a jealous God, punishing the children for the sin of the fathers to the third and fourth generation of those who hate me, but showing love to a thousand (generations) of those who love me and keep my commandments.

"You shall not misuse the name of the LORD your God, for the LORD will not hold anyone guiltless who misuses his name.

"Remember the Sabbath day by keeping it holy. Six days you shall labour and do all your work, but the seventh day is a Sabbath to the LORD your God. On it you shall not do any work, neither you, nor your son or daughter, nor your manservant or maidservant, nor your animals, nor the alien within your gates. For in six days the LORD made the heavens and the earth, the sea, and all that is in them, but he rested on the seventh day. Therefore the LORD blessed the Sabbath day and made it holy.

"Honour your father and your mother, so that you may live long in the land the LORD your God is giving you.

"You shall not murder.

"You shall not commit adultery.

"You shall not steal.

"You shall not give false testimony against your neighbour.

"You shall not covet your neighbour's house. You shall not covet your neighbour's wife, or his manservant or maidservant, his ox or donkey, or anything that belongs to your neighbour." (NIVUK)

Next has to be one of the strangest verses of the whole Bible... The people don't actually "want" to relate to God Himself—but only have Moses do it for them, when this was the one thing the Lord really wanted—fellowship—everyone a priest...

> Vs 18-23 When the people saw the thunder and lightning and heard the trumpet and saw the mountain in smoke, they trembled with fear. They stayed at a distance and said to Moses, "Speak to us yourself and we will listen. But do not have God speak to us or we will die."
>
> Moses said to the people, "Do not be afraid. God has come to test you, so that the fear of God will be with you to keep you from sinning."
>
> The people remained at a distance, while Moses approached the thick darkness where God was. (NIV)

And after more promises and instructions in chapter 23 we arrive at Exodus 24:3

> When Moses went and told the people all the LORD's words and laws, they responded with one voice, "Everything the LORD has said we will do." Moses then wrote down everything the LORD had said. (NIV)

And now we arrive at the initiation of this covenant between God and the Israelites: a sacrifice, and the shedding and sprinkling of blood, a reading of the terms of the covenant, and the people's agreement.

> Exodus 24:4-8 He got up early the next morning and built an altar at the foot of the mountain and set up twelve stone pillars representing the twelve tribes of Israel. Then he sent young Israelite men,

153

and they offered burnt offerings and sacrificed young bulls as fellowship offerings to the LORD. Moses took half of the blood and put it in bowls, and the other half he sprinkled on the altar. Then he took the Book of the Covenant and read it to the people. They responded, "We will do everything the LORD has said; we will obey."

Moses then took the blood, sprinkled it on the people and said, "This is the blood of the covenant that the LORD has made with you in accordance with all these words." (NIV)

Now do a double-check with this completion of the whole occasion…

Vs 9-11, Moses and Aaron, Nadab and Abihu, and the seventy elders of Israel went up **and saw the God of Israel**. Under his feet was something like a pavement made of sapphire, clear as the sky itself. But God did not raise his hand against these leaders of the Israelites; they saw God, and they ate and drank. (NIV) (emphasis mine)

So here is the Covenant meal (feast) between God and representatives of the people.

Now you probably skipped over it as a familiar verse from back in Exodus. But just go back and read it again. Seventy-five people "*saw the God of Israel*". We probably remember Moses being stuck in a cleft of the rock, while God revealed Himself and passed by, but here, in this episode, the whole group saw Him. And just stop and think for a moment at that description of the pavement under His feet. This really is something quite extraordinary.

Vs 12, The LORD said to Moses, "Come up to me on the mountain and stay here, and I will give you the tablets of stone, with the law and commands I have written for their instruction."

And here are the tablets of stone—the written record of the agreement—just like the title deeds of your house. Here is the physical memorial—and as was often the case in such a covenant—each partner put their part side by side with the other's. So inside the ark of the covenant, it is proposed, are two identical tablets—not five words on one and five words on the other, but ten on each. One tablet is Moses' on behalf of the people and one is for the Lord. (A check on the Hebrew does not reveal this, but I have heard it said that each commandment was summed by a single Hebrew word.)

All the Key Ingredients of Covenant

The corollary is the making of the tabernacle and all of the priestly garments and further spelling out of the law and what's right and wrong—but here in Exodus, chapter 24, is the cutting of this Old Covenant agreement.

There are many other wonderful and strange events there in the wilderness, but for now we are looking purely at the initiation of the Old Covenant—as we need to compare and contrast with the initiation of the New Covenant—and the similarities and differences between the two.

The Patriarchal Covenants

Parallels	Abraham Genesis 15	Abraham Genesis 17	Isaac Genesis 26	Joseph Genesis 28
The parties: The Lord &	Abraham	Abraham	Isaac	Jacob
The conditions	Unconditional	Circumcision vs 10	Unconditional	Unconditional
The Terms		If you keep circumcision vs 10	Stay in Gerar and don't go down to Egypt vs 2	
The Sign	He saw the Lord pass between the pieces	Birth of Isaac vs 16	Reaped a hundredfold vs 12	If he returned home vs 21
The Promises	The Land of Canaan as a permanent inheritance	Father of Many Nations vs 4 Canaan for an everlasting possession vs 8	I AM with thee I will bless thee I will multiply thy seed In thy seed shall all the nations of the earth be blessed.	The land you are I will give to your seed vs 14 The Lord would be with him and keep him, and bring him back again. vs 15
The shedding of blood	Animal Blood Sacrifice Vs 9	None	None	None
The Celebratory feast	The Lord passed between the laid out carcasses vs 17	None	None	None
The Physical Memorial	His children being as numerous as the number of the stars and the number of the grains of sand	Birth of Isaac	He Built an Altar The name of the well- 'The well of Covenant'	Set up a Pillar calling the place Bethel vs 18

Comparing the Abrahamic, Old & New Covenants

Parallels	Abraham Genesis 15	Old Covenant Exodus 19-20, 24	New Covenant
The parties: The Lord &	Abraham	All Israel: a Kingdom of Priests vs 6	All Believers: a royal priesthood, a holy nation, 1 Peter 2:9; i.e. a Kingdom of Priests
The conditions	Unconditional	The 10 Commandments Exodus 20	Receiving Jesus as your personal Redeemer
The Terms	Take the animals for sacrifice.. vs 9	If you Obey	Fulfilled by Jesus on our behalf
The Sign	He saw the Lord pass between the pieces	Circumcision	Circumcision of the heart
The Promises	The Land of Canaan as a permanent inheritance	Out of all nations you will be my treasured possession. Although the whole earth is mine, you will be for me a kingdom of priests and a holy nation.	Full redemption from sin. Made a New Creation. Adoption into the Father's family. Right standing before God.
The shedding of blood	Blood Sacrifice vs 9	Blood sacrifice Exodus 24:5 & 6	Jesus' blood, "once and for all"
The Celebratory feast	The Lord alone, passed between the laid out carcasses vs 17	Exodus 24:11 The leaders saw God and did eat and drink.	The Last Supper
The Physical Memorial	The number of his children being as the number of the stars and grains of sand	The tablets in the Ark of the Covenant.	The cross and the empty tomb
The Memorial Reminder	Unto thy seed have I given this land, from the river of Egypt unto the great river,	The Passover celebration	"This is the blood of the New Covenant, Do this in remembrance of Me"

Conclusion

Most stirring for me is that ALL of the Old Covenant promises are now the property of the New Covenant believer. The promises are the same.

The difference is in the conditions, in that Jesus has fulfilled absolutely and to the letter, all of the terms on our behalf.

So if the Lord has promised it, then He can't say "No—you can't have it."

Or as Paul wrote to the Corinthians: 2 Corinthians 1:20, For **all** the **promises** of **God** in him are yea, and in him Amen, unto the glory of **God** by us. (emphasis mine)

Chapter 23
The Fulfilment of the Old Covenant

Many have studied and drawn up types and parallels between the Old Covenant and the life and crucifixion of Jesus. I only propose to scratch the surface here, leaving you to delve deeper for yourself. I owe much to Matthew Byrne[1] again, for the detail of the Last Supper and its Passover origins.

So many of the ideas I bring out here are precious revelation the Lord has given to others. May they bless and encourage you as they have me!

> Luke 24:44 And he said unto them, "These are the words which I spake unto you, while I was yet with you, that all things must be fulfilled, which were written in the law of Moses, and in the prophets, and in the psalms, concerning me."

So much of the Law was describing prophetically the events that Jesus would ultimately fulfil for our Redemption. When you grind to a halt in your reading of the Bible then start looking for those prophetic descriptions of Calvary. Genesis is good story-telling on into Exodus, but by the time you hit Leviticus you will be seriously wondering why you tried this. Well, see how each of the different sacrifices are so similar— they are all descriptions of the same one, "Once and for all" sacrifice of Jesus. His sacrifice of Himself encompassed them all. His sacrifice was a sin offering, but it was also a peace offering and a love offering and the list could go on. But also

---

[1] The Day He Died – Columba Press ISBN 1-85607-430-7

much of what the prophets wrote equally described Jesus' sacrifice, such as Isaiah, chapter 53. Now Isaiah's account is in many ways more graphic than the Gospel accounts as his description is from the perspective of heaven. It would be so easy to stop there, but Jesus also includes the psalmists. And of course there are many graphic accounts there too, especially that most gruesome of all, Psalm 22, which Jesus Himself was speaking as He hung there. As men despised Him and laughed Him to scorn, parting his garments among them and casting lots for them, His bones were indeed "out of joint". Crucifixion does that.

Was the Old Covenant fully and truly fulfilled? Oh Yes! But there is only one way we can know this—by Jesus' Resurrection. That is why this is just so significant.

> Exodus 12:3 Tell the whole community of Israel that on the tenth day of this month each man is to take a lamb for his family, one for each household. (NIV)

> Exodus 12:6 Take care of them until the fourteenth day of the month, when all the people of the community of Israel must slaughter them at twilight. (NIV)

This little insignificant detail is so easily missed, but typical of the wonder of the parallels to uncover. The lamb was chosen on the tenth day of the month and brought into the household as a household pet until the fourteenth day. Just long enough for the children to have become seriously attached to it. Dare we ever forget just how precious Jesus was and always will be to the Father—*"His Beloved Son in whom He is well pleased!"*[2]

And Jesus himself paralleled this in his entry into

---

[2] Mark 1:11

Jerusalem with all of the crowd cheering Him on, on the tenth day of the month. He entered into what should have been His reign, as the crowd hung on His every word, as He taught in the temple. He was the crowd's chosen one—chosen by the sinner, and the common people.

And He was sacrificed on the fourteenth day of the month—just when all of the sacrificial lambs for the Jews to celebrate Passover, were slaughtered.

Have you ever wondered how come the disciples were happy to arrange and celebrate the Passover meal the day before the real Passover? When Passover falls on a Sabbath then there's a problem of conflict between the two. One of the solutions is to celebrate the Passover a day early, which is exactly what happened that fateful Passover. So the disciples would have been perfectly familiar with this and it would have been of no consequence to them. For those who celebrated on the correct day, they were sacrificing their lambs at the very same moment as The Sacrificial Lamb hung there. Such is the parallel.

Passover Parallels

Pharaoh downwards paid a heavy price for their refusal to acknowledge the Lord's Lordship. This is the price that we "should" each have to pay, were it not for the real Passover fulfilment at Calvary.

The Meal was prepared in haste—what a reflection of the hasty pressure to see Jesus crucified—sweeping through all of the normal provisions of justice.

The Lamb—one for a house—one Lamb for our whole world.

Not a bone of its body must be broken—not one bone of His body was broken.

Conclusion

Jesus is the true sacrificial lamb, that Passover had pointed to for so long.

He fulfilled ALL the law and the prophets.

All God's promises are YES and Amen in HIM.

This is our God of Mercy.

Appendix 1
The value of the Household Gods

In the culture and law at the time of the Patriarchs, the owner of the household gods held the birthright. They were the title deeds for the inheritance. This is behind Rachel's taking Laban's household gods when Jacob finally decided to leave Laban to return to his family, in Genesis 31.

> Genesis 31:14-16 And Rachel and Leah answered and said unto him, Is there yet any portion or inheritance for us in our father's house? Are we not counted of him strangers? for he hath sold us, and hath quite devoured also our money. For all the riches which God hath taken from our father, that is ours, and our children's: now then, whatsoever God hath said unto thee, do.

See how concerned they were that they had no inheritance to take with them? Jacob had a rather better understanding that we would do well to appreciate—that his inheritance was given him by the Lord, and he didn't have to take or steal from anyone.

> Vs 19, And Laban went to shear his sheep: and Rachel had stolen the images that were her father's. (emphasis mine)

Next we see how desperate Laban is to get those idols back. He was so desperate that the Lord had to speak to him to make sure he didn't harm Jacob:

> Vs 22-37, And it was told Laban on the third day that Jacob was fled. And he took his brethren with him, and pursued after him seven days' journey; and they overtook him in the mount Gilead. And God came to Laban the Syrian in a dream by night, and said unto him, Take heed that thou speak not to Jacob either good or bad. Then Laban overtook Jacob. Now Jacob had pitched his tent in the mount: and Laban with his brethren pitched in the mount of Gilead.
>
> And Laban said to Jacob, "What hast thou done, that thou hast stolen away unawares to me, and carried away my daughters, as captives taken with the sword? Wherefore didst thou flee away secretly, and steal away from me; and didst not tell me, that I might have sent thee away with mirth, and with songs, with tabret, and with harp? And hast not suffered me to kiss my sons and my daughters? thou hast now done foolishly in so doing. It is in the power of my hand to do you hurt: but the God of your father spake unto me yesternight, saying, Take thou heed that thou speak not to Jacob either good or bad. And now, though thou wouldest needs be gone, because thou sore longedst after thy father's house, yet wherefore hast thou stolen my gods?"
>
> Now Rachel had taken the images, and put them in the camel's furniture, and sat upon them. And Laban searched all the tent, but found them not. And she said to her father, "Let it not displease my lord that I cannot rise up before thee; for the

custom of women is upon me." And he searched but found not the images.

And Jacob was wroth, and chode with Laban: and Jacob answered and said to Laban, "What is my trespass? what is my sin, that thou hast so hotly pursued after me? Whereas thou hast searched all my stuff, what hast thou found of all thy household stuff? set it here before my brethren and thy brethren, that they may judge betwixt us both."

Rachel paid dearly for taking these household gods rather than trusting the Lord. She died giving birth to her next child.

Genesis 35:16-20 And they journeyed from Bethel; and there was but a little way to come to Ephrath: and Rachel travailed, and she had hard labour. And it came to pass, when she was in hard labour, that the midwife said unto her, Fear not; thou shalt have this son also. And it came to pass, as her soul was in departing, (for she died) that she called his name Benoni: but his father called him Benjamin. And Rachel died, and was buried in the way to Ephrath, which is Bethlehem. And Jacob set a pillar upon her grave: that is the pillar of Rachel's grave unto this day.

Appendix 2
The Life of Abraham and Sarah

The story of Abram and the promises the Lord made to him are absolutely fascinating and well-studied. Though scarcely central to the theme, it is hardly complete without my own personal exploration of the life of Abram—becoming Abraham.

It is a great relief to know that in all our failings, our tripping-up and falling on our faces, these are not recorded for posterity to rub our noses in, only our successes. Abraham and Sarah made plenty of mistakes, as told in Genesis, but in the roll call in the book of Hebrews, chapter 11, none of these are recorded; only their faith that the Lord would fulfil what He had promised.

> The call: Genesis 12:1-5 Now the LORD had said unto Abram, "Get thee out of thy country, and from thy kindred, and from thy father's house, unto a land that I will shew thee: and I will make of thee a great nation, and I will bless thee, and make thy name great; and thou shalt be a blessing: and I will bless them that bless thee, and curse him that curseth thee: and in thee shall all families of the earth be blessed."

> So Abram departed, as the LORD had spoken unto him; and Lot went with him: and Abram was seventy and five years old when he departed out of Haran. And Abram took Sarai his wife, and Lot his brother's son, and all their substance that they had gathered, and the souls that they had gotten in Haran; and they went forth to go into the land of Canaan; and into the land of Canaan they came.

I so like Danny Silk's comments on this in his book *Culture of Honour*.[1] Abram had to leave behind all the familiar things that defined him and inadvertently set his limitations. So often we too need to leave our comfort zone to step into all the Lord has for us.

But Abram wasn't told where to go—it was almost as though that wasn't important.

"And leave his family"…few things define who we are, and thereby set our limitations, as much as our family.

And even then he wasn't obedient as he took Lot with him.

Cutting the Covenant

> Genesis 15:7-18 And he said unto him, "I am the Lord that brought thee out of Ur of the Chaldees, to give thee this land to inherit it."
>
> And he said, "Lord God, whereby shall I know that I shall inherit it?"
>
> And he said unto him, "Take me an heifer of three years old, and a she goat of three years old, and a ram of three years old, and a turtledove, and a young pigeon."
>
> And he took unto him all these, and divided them in the midst, and laid each piece one against another: but the birds divided he not. And when the fowls came down upon the carcases, Abram drove them away.
>
> And when the sun was going down, a deep sleep fell upon Abram; and, lo, an horror of great darkness fell upon him… And it came to pass, that, when the sun went down, and it was dark, behold a

---

[1] Culture of Honour – Chapter 5 - Four Keys to New Freedom

smoking furnace, and a burning lamp that passed between those pieces.

In the same day the Lord made a covenant with Abram, saying, Unto thy seed have I given this land, from the river of Egypt unto the great river, the river Euphrates.

Now, two parties cutting covenant this way would normally walk between the pieces together. But this is an unconditional covenant; God alone walks between the pieces laid out on the ground. That promise there in verse 18 is an unconditional, covenanted promise.

The Blood Covenant: Genesis 17

When Abram and Sarai are given their new names, evidently Abram recognised who this person was who was talking to him. I don't think Abram was the kind of person to fall on his face in front of anyone.

The words out of our mouths are so very important. Our words are spiritual containers—they carry life and power. It is not really surprising that the Lord had to change their names for the promise of Isaac to become a reality.

Sarai means "barren", and she becomes Sarah—or "Princess". So through all of those years Abram has simply been re-enforcing Sarai's barrenness.

Abram becomes "The Father of Many Nations"—I think the household servants must have had a good laugh over that one, without a proper heir to his name. Many times familiarity in a story like this masks the reality for those involved.

If you are reading this and praying for a child—read on. The child is yours, courtesy of a binding Blood Covenant with an ALL MIGHTY GOD, but like Abram and Sarai get your confession full of faith and expectancy, from this day on.

Consider it a done deal. When the pregnancy test shows positive what do you now call each other but Mum and Dad. Can you change your names for each other to Mum and Dad, ahead of that—now in your faith and trust in HIM? It would be easy for this to be seen as presumption, when really it is a serious reminder to yourselves and to Him of your trust in His promise. For many wrestling in this area I fully recognise this is a painful thing to do, which for me rather heightens the deep reality behind it.

Over the years, I have shared this very specifically and intentionally and I know of at least one couple who got the message, applied it, and now have a family.

The Promises:

Genesis 17:6-8 "And I will make thee exceeding fruitful, and I will make nations of thee, and kings shall come out of thee. And I will establish my covenant between me and thee and thy seed after thee in their generations for an everlasting covenant, to be a God unto thee, and to thy seed after thee. And I will give unto thee, and to thy seed after thee, the land wherein thou art a stranger, all the land of Canaan, for an everlasting possession; and I will be their God."

Note that this is an everlasting covenant.

The Covenant Conditions:
Genesis 17:10-12—Circumcision

> Vs 15-17 And God said unto Abraham, "As for Sarai thy wife, thou shalt not call her name Sarai, but Sarah shall her name be. And I will bless her, and give thee a son also of her: yea, I will bless

her, and she shall be a mother of nations; kings of people shall be of her.

Then Abraham fell upon his face, and laughed, and said in his heart, "Shall a child be born unto him that is an hundred years old? and shall Sarah, that is ninety years old, bear?"

So it wasn't only Sarah who laughed at the idea of Sarah bearing a son.

In zipping through Abraham's life we then come to an amazing episode in Genesis 18.

The Visit:

The visit by the three men:

Genesis 18:2, Three men stood by him, and he recognised them and called them "My Lord".

Note in this context verses 16-17 that the men left to go to Sodom, and the Lord stayed and talked to Abraham. The rest of chapter 18 is clearly a conversation between Abraham and the Lord—this is easily understood. But the two men when they arrive at Sodom in Genesis 19:1 are now referred to as angels, or messengers and are addressed and worshiped by Lot as God Himself. Now remember that angels would very quickly put a stop to that. So are these two Jesus and Holy Spirit?

Note on their arrival how keen and quick Abraham is to "run" to the flock to fetch a tender and good calf, and instructed Sarah to get on with doing her bit making some bread. He knew to honour these guests.

And like so many others, I do so love it that when now at last the Lord spells out the timeframe for her to have a son, Sarah laughs. But this is not met with any put-down or condemnation for her unbelief, just that wonderful retort of verse 15, "Oh, but you did laugh."

Now this is Earth's account and description, but turn forward a few pages to the description of Sarah as that mighty warrior of faith given by the writer to the Hebrews, for this is Heaven's record:

> Hebrews 11:11 Through faith also Sara herself received strength to conceive seed, and was delivered of a child when she was past age, because she judged him faithful who had promised.

Oh, there's hope for you and me yet. "He is faithful who promised."

In the context of Abraham and Sarah, we skip over the account of Sodom and Gomorrah and join Abraham once again at the court of Abimilech: Genesis 20.

A whole chapter is devoted to this crazy episode, right at the most crucial moment in the story. The Lord has just visited Abraham and Sarah and reminded them that Sarah will have a son within the year—in spite of Sarah's laughter at the very idea. Abraham then moves to the South and Sarah enters the harem of the local king Abimilech. Now surely this is hardly a good way to increase their love-making time. And what on earth does Abimilech see in an eighty-nine-year-old woman to want her in his harem? In the previous few chapters her age has been well and truly spelled out and emphasized and here she is entering his harem.

God then confronts Abimilech in a dream and scares the daylights out of him. Now this is quite reasonable from God's perspective, for if Abimilech had sexual relations with Sarah there would be all the controversy as to whether Abraham or Abimilech were the real father of Isaac. So Abimilech has to go through a host of totally unreasonable steps to prove beyond all doubt that nothing ever transpired between him and Sarah.

But just how long was Sarah in the harem? Well, it can't

have been more than three months as she had to be back with Abraham in time for him to sire Isaac who was born a year after the visitation described in chapter 17. But what is very curious is the comment that Abraham then prays for Abimilech's household who had been made barren by the arrival in their midst of barren Sarah—she seemed to take her barrenness with her.

But so often our Redeemer changes a situation around when we repent and ask Him to forgive us and sort it out, so it almost seems like He planned it all along. I rather think the fecundity of Abimilech's harem rubbed off, and was probably rather needful into Sarah's heart, vision and attitude. If you are friends with anyone struggling for years to have a family, you will know that it leads to great stress, anticipation, and anticlimax as each month passes. It readily becomes very counterproductive. What kind of a household recognizes that they are struck by barrenness after a couple of months? It has to be one that is abounding in pregnancies, so that this is seriously the order of the day—of every day. What kind of a culture shock would this represent to Sarah? Just what she needed.

Conclusion

We really have to laugh at the absurdities of this story—just what do Abraham and Sarah think they are doing? To me this does not read like one believing "Him faithful who had promised".[2]

So there is indeed hope for you and me.

Through all of our doubts, failings and misgivings—"He is faithful that promised, to complete that which He started in you."[3] While He certainly expects our cooperation, there is so much we cannot do. While Abraham and Sarah had much lovemaking to do to sire Isaac, it wasn't lost on them that after all of those years that was never going to be enough.

The crazy part is, that when He fixes things, He does it all so naturally you blink and miss His involvement that made it all happen. We're busy looking for signs or the flashes and stars flying from the magic wand…but that is just not His way.

Can we allow Him to be God? Can we allow Him to be Himself, and do things His way, while we trust in His ability to fulfil His promises?

How easy it is to try to humanly engineer the fulfilment we have been asking for, just as Abram and Sarai landed themselves with Ishmael—a serious problem for the child of the promise.

---

[2] Hebrews 11:11
[3] Philippians 1:6

Recommended Additional Reading

The Blood Covenant   Dr E.W Kenyon

What Happened from the Cross to the Throne   Dr E.W. Kenyon

The Blood and the Glory   Billye Brim

ALL of Bill Johnson's wonderful books, such as
When Heaven Invades Earth
The Supernatural Power of a Transformed Mind
Hosting the Presence
Releasing the Spirit of Prophecy
Experience the Impossible
Strengthen Yourself in the Lord

School of the Prophets   Kris Vallotten

Culture of Honor   Danny Silk

The Day He Died – The Passion according to Luke
                    Mathew Byrne

About the Author

Jim Edwards is a passionate lover of Jesus, He lives on the South Coast of the UK, with his wife Val. They celebrated their 40th wedding anniversary this year, 2016. They have four amazing and wonderful children.

As Technical Sales Manager for a high voltage power supply company he has made regular visits to his USA customers and on to Bethel Church in Redding California. The role is to explain the details of the electronics to technical and non-technical people alike. Now remember, you cannot see electrons, so the role translates to that of explaining the operation and details of things that you cannot see, to a wide variety of people.

His hope and prayer is that you have encountered Father, Jesus, and Holy Spirit through this book. They love you dearly, and long to bless you outrageously. Jim would always love to hear that story. He can be contacted via Edwards Family Publishing on Facebook.

This is the second of a number of books, there are more to follow—watch this space.

Additional Books by the Author:

Your Invitation

Now where should a Passion Play end?

Good Friday is over and the tomb closed and sealed.

Eavesdrop on a group whose play doesn't end where their scriptwriter intended.

Join them for their Easter service, and travel with them, as they experience for themselves the resurrection appearances of Jesus.

Did Jesus really rise from the dead? Does it matter? Is it of any relevance for us? How would you recognize Him? What would it look like, if He were to come back today? How could He help you?

Then share in their very personal invitation to a life-changing encounter.

This is *Your Invitation*.

ISBN-13: 978-1497403086

ISBN-10: 1497403081

Amazon ref: 'Your Invitation'   James Victor Edwards

Print: www.amazon.com/Your-Invitation-Mr-James-Edwards/dp/1497403081

Kindle: ASIN: B00BTNGYM0

176

Living and Breathing the Psalms

Living and Breathing the Psalms is a raw and very personal prayer journey.

Here are the Old Covenant prayers, poems and songs to the Lord, reframed through intimacy and relationship with each member of the Trinity. From this perspective the Psalms break open in a simple, fresh and dynamic way.

Key life themes lie in these ancient songs of worship, at the very heart of Old Covenant experience, belief and ritual. Exploring them, we find them unlocked through an intimate relationship with our Saviour and King, Firstborn Son of our Heavenly Papa God, as revealed to us by Holy Spirit.

Here, unashamedly viewed through faith and trust in Mighty King Jesus, Mashiach, the Anointed One, is pain, hurt and grief, side by side with fire, passion, love, thanks, praise and worship.

As you put your trust, hope and faith in Him, may you find here your heart's cries to our High King of Heaven and Earth.

Available from Amazon   Print & Kindle
ISBN-13: 978-1535590730
ISBN-10: 1535590734
Kindle ASIN: B01LOZL5MQ

Living and Breathing Romans to Galatians

Living and Breathing Romans to Galatians is an easy reading paraphrase of the Epistles. Here are Paul's early letters to these embryonic early churches.

Guarded, and carefully copied through the centuries for us, they are now unravelled in a fresh way, in the everyday language of today. They are here amplified to explain the revelation Paul personally received from Jesus that he was so concerned to share with all who would receive it. Here is Paul's heart revealed, alongside the price he paid to share this Good News of Jesus.

Here is the Good News that the same Holy Spirit who anointed Jesus wants to live in you, to strengthen you and demonstrate with signs and wonders through you that Jesus is our Redeemer and Father God's Anointed Son.

The reality of the promises, the prayers and the truths of this wonderful Good News that Jesus paid such a high price to bring us, is vibrantly brought to life. While Holy Spirit's life-changing, heart-changing, healing power to comfort, to save, to deliver, to restore, and to bring hope is here laid out for us.

Alongside the text, are thought provoking study questions, notes and cross references, to unveil the enormity of all that Jesus won for us, and to reveal our Heavenly Father's wondrous heart of love; His longing to know and be known, by us all.

Available from Amazon   Print

ISBN-13: 978-1727130621
ISBN-10: 1727139626
Kindle ASIN: Not yet available.

This is the companion volume to *Living and Breathing Hebrews to Jude.*

Living &
Breathing
Romans
to
Galatians

Jim Edwards

Living and Breathing Ephesians to Philemon

Living and Breathing Ephesians to Philemon is an easy reading paraphrase of these Epistles. Here are Paul's letters to these embryonic early churches; many written from prison, and a couple shortly before he was martyred.

Guarded, and carefully copied through the centuries for us, they are now unravelled in a fresh way, in the everyday language of the twenty-first century. They are here amplified to explain the revelation Paul personally received from Jesus that he was so concerned to share with all who would receive it. Here is Paul's heart revealed, with his instructions and encouragement to his closest friends and co-workers. Here are his descriptions of a life Anointed by Holy Spirit who wants to live in us, to strengthen you and I to demonstrate with signs and wonders through us that Jesus is our Redeemer and Father God's Anointed Son, and Lord of All..

The reality of the promises, the prayers and the truths of this wonderful Good News that Jesus paid such a high price to bring us, is vibrantly brought to life. While Holy Spirit's anointing, to bring life-changing, heart-changing, healing power to comfort, to save, to deliver, to restore, and to bring hope is here laid out.

Alongside the text, are thought provoking study questions, notes and cross references, to unveil the enormity of all that Jesus won for us, and to reveal our Heavenly Father's wondrous heart of love; His longing to know and be known, by us all.

Available from Amazon   Print
ISBN-10: 1704705959
ISBN-13: 9781704705958
Kindle ASIN: Not yet available.

This is the companion volume to *Living and Breathing Romans to Galatians* and *Living and Breathing Hebrews to Jude*.

Living and Breathing Hebrews to Jude

Living and Breathing Hebrews to Jude is an easy reading paraphrase of the Epistles. Here are letters written to us from those who knew Jesus intimately, who were brought up with Him, or spent years with Him as His disciples.

Guarded, and carefully copied through the centuries for us, they are now unravelled in a fresh way, in the everyday language of the twenty-first century. They are here amplified to explain the truths those early followers of Jesus were so concerned to pass on to their fellow believers.

The reality of the promises, the prayers and the truths of the wonderful good news that Jesus paid such a high price to bring us, is vibrantly brought to life. While Holy Spirit's life-changing, heart-changing, healing power to comfort, to save, to deliver, to restore, and to bring hope is here laid out for us.

Alongside the text, are thought provoking study questions, notes and cross references, to unveil the enormity of all that Jesus won for us, and to reveal our Heavenly Father's wondrous heart of love; His longing to know and be known, by us all.

Available from Amazon   Print & Kindle
ISBN-13: 978-1979871358
ISBN-10: 1979871353
Kindle ASIN: BO8VW0G0ZT

This is the companion volume to *Living and Breathing Romans to Galatians,* and *Living and Breathing Ephesians to Philemon.*

Living &
Breathing
Hebrews
to Jude

Jim Edwards

Coming soon

Summoned:

to a life of intimacy with the King of Glory

You are summoned to a life of intimacy with the High King of Heaven.
You! Yes *YOU*!
Why and how do we respond to such a call and what does it look like?
He only knows to love at any cost; will you too give up anything less.
He only knows to trust in hope and faith, and *you*.

It takes the blink of an eye and it takes a lifetime.
You gain—your destiny—your dreams—your significance.
It costs nothing, but yet it costs everything i.e.
Your destiny—your dreams—your significance
What does it cost Him, and what does He gain?
He is not thirsty for worship, but He is thirsty for relationship with
you, and for you and me freely wanting to relate to Him.

Do you accept His summons and your assignment?
Sounds impossibly hard? It starts with you simply saying 'Yes'.
He will make the next move—trust me!

As the best of fathers, He will speak so that you hear,
And every response, He always gives you the awesome freedom to choose.

ISBN-13:978-1536912357
ISBN-10:1536912352

John316Network

For other independent Christian authors, search for the John316Network, founded by Lorilyn Roberts.

These authors cover every genre, with members from many nations, but all with a Christian worldview.

Check out Lorilyn's award winning 'Seventh Dimension' series. This series is just so much more than a YA Fantasy.

While unable here, to endorse all of their books, or even all of the network, such authors, in totally random order, include

Lisa Lickel
Emma & Guy Right
Nicola Taylor
Martin Roth
Dana Rongione
Angelique McGlotton
Barbara Derksen
Roberto Roche
Carole Brown
Laura Davis
Trish Jenkins
Janis Cox
Anita Estes

Jerry Jenkins
Tracy Krauss
Katherine Harms
Carol Brown
Alice Wisler
Pamela Carmichael
Elizabeth Paige
Randy Kirk
Cheryl Colwell
Joseph Young
Carol Round
Malo Bel
Deborah Bateman

Made in the USA
Middletown, DE
23 May 2021

40014401R00109